Taking Faith to Work

Next Steps for Christian Discipleship

PAUL M. MINUS

Centered Life
Luther Seminary
2481 Como Ave.
St. Paul, MN 55108

Except where noted, direct Scripture notations are from the Holy
Bible: Revised Standard Version. Copyright 1946, 1952, 1959, 1973
by the Division of Christian Education of the National Council of
the Churches of Christ in the United States of America.

For additional copies of this book or to learn more about
Centered Life, contact us at 651-641-3444 or visit our Web site at
www.centeredlife.org.

Printed in the United States of America.

ISBN 09742283-4-6

To the Memory of
Carolyn Dickerson Minus, 1941-1994
Christian Layperson *Extraordinaire*

Contents

Introduction

"The movement away from ministry as the monopoly of ordained men to ministry as the responsibility of the whole people of God, ordained as well as non-ordained, is one of the most dramatic shifts taking place in the church today."
David J. Bosch, 1991[1]

A powerful conviction is emerging among Christians in this country and around the world. They increasingly recognize that God is summoning followers of Christ to take faith to work, so that the gospel can come alive in workplaces and institutions having little room for faith, hope, and love.

Make no mistake: This is no easy task, and much still needs to be learned about how to perform it well. But as I have found from two decades of exploring this frontier with lay and clergy friends, the connecting of faith and work—Sunday and Monday—belongs at the center of the Christian life. That is so because this connecting task expresses something fundamental about God's gracious design for the world and for us. It also responds to an eagerness more and more evident today among people in all manner of workplaces for a way to give their daily labor dignity and meaning. And, as we shall see, the evidence grows that resourceful, persistent effort to bridge faith and work can bear fruit in the lives of the people who build these bridges, in the institutions where they work, and in the congregations that support their effort.

I have written this little book partly as a guide for those in the early stages of travel down this road, and partly as an invitation to others who have not yet left their familiar places. As I have talked with people at different stages of this journey, I have heard again and again how energizing it can be, both for those well down the road and for those just starting out.

I also have discovered how diverse are the people (and their workplace situations) who want to make the faith-work connection. Here are a few I have been privileged to know (real people with made-up names):

- Steve, the owner of a small public relations firm tempted to bend the rules in order to keep his business afloat
- Kathy, the housecleaner seeking relief from the boredom of her job
- Jean, the young mother hard-pressed to cope with the growing demands of an enjoyable job and her responsibilities to her children and husband
- Dave, the VP of a Fortune 500 bank looking to his faith for help in keeping himself and his department on a steady course in a time of enormous competitive pressure and personal stress
- Susan, the Army captain seeking a role for "spirituality" in the military
- Tim, the motel desk clerk wondering how much longer he can bear the badgering of his boss
- Hae-Lim, the seventh-grader hoping her confirmation class will shed light on her choice of a career
- Ricardo, the economics instructor in a state university searching for the gospel's bearing upon his teaching and writing
- Jill, the high school math teacher eager to do something about the moral drift among many of her students
- Andy, the recently retired lawyer looking for a useful volunteer role in the community
- Emily, the newly installed pastor of a suburban church eager to overcome her predecessors' disinterest in helping parishioners connect faith and work
- John, the state legislator aspiring to higher office and wider service but wondering about the costs to his family and to his own soul
- Stacy, the single-parent mom laid off from her secretarial job and worrying about a chronic health problem

The listing of so diverse a group suggests just how inclusive is the circle of Christians challenged to connect faith and work. In fact, my understanding of the gospel leads me to believe that all Christians who work are called by God to pursue this connecting task. No worker or workplace is exempt. Included are those with jobs in a wide range of traditional workplaces, such as the waitress, the computer technician, the accountant, the CEO, the plumber, the sales representative, the artist, the engineer, the checkout clerk, the research scientist, the mechanic, the journalist, the mail carrier.

And, at a time of shifting patterns and understandings of work, also included are those involved in places not normally thought of as workplaces: the management consultant operating from a home office, the student in school, the retiree volunteering in a nonprofit organization, the homemaker managing a household, the pastor serving a congregation, the professional soccer player, and the like.

From the perspective of Christian faith, our workplace is wherever we spend a significant portion of our time, engaged in activity (whether compensated or not) that produces goods and services, that makes use of our God-given talents, and that provides us an opportunity to serve God's purposes for the world.

In the pages that follow, I shall explain this vision of the Sunday-Monday connection in a way that combines the richness of biblical faith, the tough realities of everyday life, and the stories of American Catholics and Protestants effectively making the connection (comparable stories, not told here, are also emerging among Christians elsewhere in the world). I have deliberately made this a brief book, so that busy people can easily read through it and reflect upon it. I hope its message will move them to new clarity, commitment, and action. I also hope that those readers engaged in a study process with others will find adequate assistance here to help them explore this message productively. They are especially pointed to the section at the end (beginning on page 97), where various teaching and learning aids, geared to individual chapters, are included.

A word of appreciation is now due the many people who have helped me discover work as a prime arena of Christian discipleship. Through most of my adult life as a teacher at the Methodist Theological School in Ohio, I taught and wrote about the twentieth-century renewal movements that were seeking to make the church more alive to God and thus better able to serve God's intentions for the human family. One of the most important of these movements was the pursuit of lay discipleship in the world of work. But it was not until a later stage of my career, when in 1986 I became the founding president of the Council for Ethics in Economics, that I plunged into the daily responsibilities of management and began interacting regularly with Christian laypeople who were eager for help in relating their faith to their workplace roles. Then I saw the enormous potential of an awakened laity deliberately serving God in workplaces in this country and around the world. That is a vision which, once having been seen, can not be unseen!

This book constitutes a report from the frontlines about what I have learned regarding the tasks God gives Christians in the workplace. Much of what is written here has been tested in lively dialogue and fruitful experimentation with lay and clergy colleagues around the country, but especially in Ohio, Massachusetts, and Connecticut.

The main thing we have learned together is this: *Each generation of Christ's disciples is called to serve God every day, in every realm of their lives. But each generation must be attentive to the particularities of God's call to them. When the first disciples heard that call, they left their workplaces to follow Christ and thereby became the nucleus of the most potent movement for personal and social transformation the world has known. Today—and as far as we can see into the twenty-first century—most of us who hear that same call will follow him best by staying in our places of work, taking up his ministry there, and living the gospel message fully.*

Chapter One

Discovering God's Call in the Workplace

Discovering God's Call in the Workplace

"We children of our time have to be the Church in a totally different world and atmosphere . . . . It is the laity, living and working in this world, which daily experiences the deep gulf between what the Church stands for and what the world drives at."
Hendrik Kraemer, 1958²

Christians have received an awesome privilege: By following Christ we become God's partners in seeking the realization of God's loving purposes for the world. Biblical writers explain this privilege in different ways, but the key point is that the church is given a critical role in helping all people know and respond to the good news and extraordinary consequences of God's mighty deeds for the world as the One who creates it, redeems it, and brings it to final fulfillment.

The record of Christians' handling of this privilege is spotty. On some fronts we and our forebears have done better, on others worse. The area of modern life where Christians have stumbled most in carrying out our mission is the workplace—the places where most of us spend a large portion of our waking hours, working for good pay, inadequate pay, or no pay; wearing white collars, blue collars, or no collars; enjoying it, hating it, or tolerating it. Here, typically, the world's self-reliance and resistance to God are most pronounced; here the testing of Christians' faithfulness to God's call to the divine-human partnership is most acute.

The present-day distance between faith and work has roots deep in the past. Since an early stage of the church's history, Christians have repeatedly been lured by alien concepts (mainly those formulated by ancient Greek philosophers) to regard their faith as having little to do with the world. Consequently, many have believed that God is found best by looking inward or upward, into the realm of spirit; they have thought that involvement in the struggles and cares of everyday life distances one from God and imperils the soul.

This "spiritualizing" of Christianity has been accompanied and reinforced by an equally regrettable "clericalizing" of the church. As early as the third century, the leadership role of clergy gradually developed in ways that departed from New Testament patterns of mutual ministry and gave clerical perspectives and interests a place of dominance in the church. There have been—and are today—many good Christian people serving as clergy, but an unfortunate consequence of long-standing clerical dominance is the fact that laypeople's perspectives and interests, significantly influenced by their daily engagement with the secular world, typically have played a secondary role in setting the church's agenda and shaping its life.[3]

 ## Exploring the Present Chasm

In modern times, with the rise of secularism, the chasm separating the realm of faith and the realm of work has grown wider and deeper. Occasionally, connections are made, but for most people today, the two worlds rarely connect. Consider:

- In many organizations an unspoken agreement exists that "religion is not spoken here." This taboo has been prompted partly by extension of the principle of church-state separation beyond the realm of its legitimate application. It has clearly been strengthened by the growing religious pluralism within American society ("we don't want to offend somebody of another faith"). One usually hears "God" and "Christ" mentioned in the workplace only by those who speak their names in anger or frustration, with no intention of making a religious point.

- The absence of faith-talk from workplaces stems also from the influence of modern economic theories attempting to explain working, buying, and selling in categories that are narrowly commercial and pay little attention to deeper human realities. For them, self-interest and profit maximization are legitimate lords of the marketplace.

- Industrial and technological development has fostered increased work specialization in organizations, pushing people to construct mental barriers between different fields and to hold narrow views of their own work roles. The tendency toward compartmentalization assigns religion to the private side of life, making it difficult for people to see its connection with such fields as business, law, and technology.

- More recently, intense global competition and economic hard times have made "lean and mean" the reigning values in many workplaces. They allow little space for such "soft" (and godly) qualities as respect and compassion.

Chief responsibility for the modern worsening of the work-faith chasm probably rests on the work side of the divide. But we must not overlook the substantial contributing role played by continuation of the church's own long-standing acceptance and reinforcement of it. So significant is this role that we shall give it major attention in a later chapter.

Fortunately, not all Christians have made their peace with the chasm. A far-seeing minority has refused to accept it.

Instead, they have mounted a determined effort to build bridges between the world of faith and the world of work.

 ## Connecting Two Worlds

The major impetus for this effort came from Europe during the middle decades of the twentieth century. At that time, especially following the devastation of World War II, thoughtful Christians from various denominational traditions began to ask what the church must do to help build a humane future in which this kind of destruction and terror never again would be unleashed. As they searched the Scriptures and their own hearts, such lay and clergy trailblazers as Joseph H. Oldham, Suzanne de Diétrich, Hendrik Kraemer, and Yves Congar concluded that, with the centuries-old culture of "Christendom" now vanquished by modern secularism, the entire church must embrace the mission of bringing the gospel to a post-Christian world.

They also agreed that this task is the mission, or ministry, bestowed by baptism on all Christians, not just clergy, for as the New Testament affirms, all have been baptized into Christ and are empowered by the Holy Spirit to serve him everyday, in every realm of life. Only by faithful implementation of this truth can Christ be recognized as the "light of the world" and Christian people fulfill their purpose as "the salt of the earth" (John 8:12; Matthew 5:13).

During the first several decades after the war, this new outlook was increasingly affirmed by leadership circles within the churches. So persuasive did it become that two summit gatherings of Christians gave it enduring expression. The first was the 1954 Evanston Assembly of the World Council of Churches:

> Lay ministry is the privilege of the whole Church . . . to share in Christ's ministry to the world. As He came to minister, so must all Christians become ministers of His saving purposes according to the gifts of the Spirit each has received . . . . It is the laity who draw together work and worship, it is they who bridge the gulf between the Church and the world . . . .

> The real battles of faith today are being fought in factories, shops, offices, and farms, in political parties and government agencies, in countless homes, in the press, radio and television, in the relationship of nations. Very often it is said the Church should "go into these spheres," but in fact the Church is already in these spheres in the persons of its laity.[4]

The Roman Catholic Church was not involved in the World Council of Churches Assembly, but ten years later, at the Second Vatican Council, Catholic bishops from around the world made a comparable affirmation of the laity's role:

> [The] laity, by their very vocation, seek the kingdom of God by engaging in temporal affairs and by ordering them according to the plan of God. They live in the world, that is in each and all the secular professions and occupations . . . . They are called there by God so that by exercising their proper function and being led by the spirit of the gospel they can work for the sanctification of the world from within, in the manner of leaven . . . .

Now, the gifts of the Spirit are diverse . . . .
He calls some to give clear witness to the desire for a
heavenly home and to keep that desire green among the
human family. He summons others to dedicate
themselves to the earthly service of men and to make
ready the material of the celestial realm by this ministry
of theirs.[5]

In the first decades following the Evanston Assembly and
Vatican II, many ecclesiastical bodies declared the importance of
lay ministry in the secular world, especially in the realm of
work. Resolute groups of Christians (mainline and Evangelical
Protestant, as well as Roman Catholic) were formed to promote
and support it. Scores of books, journals, and conferences
explored this theme.

Two observations must be made about this shift of outlook.
First, it would not have occurred without the supporting
presence of powerful new theological currents that reflected fresh
understandings of Scripture, especially regarding God's initiative
in human affairs and God's calling of the whole church to
mission in the world. Here was a compelling alternative to views
that had long supported the spiritualizing of the gospel and the
clericalizing of the church.[6] Second, this shift was a theological
development with potentially far-reaching consequences for the
everyday activity of laity and clergy—consequences that were
explored with zeal by some, but with mounting hesitancy by
others.

During the 1970s and the 1980s that hesitancy became
more and more apparent. As familiar patterns of the Christian
past began to be reasserted, this promising new movement lost
the favor it had earlier enjoyed among church leaders. However,
during the 1990s favorable winds again began to blow, perhaps
due especially to peoples' growing dissatisfaction with their
harried work lives and a hunger for more humane values in the
workplace. Renewed interest in connecting faith and work

appeared here and there within traditional ecclesiastical circles and even more strongly among new "parachurch" organizations developed beyond the familiar structures of denominations and congregations (a development to be examined in a later chapter).

Today, a curious mix is present within American Christianity. One finds numerous high-level pronouncements (mostly dating from the 1960s and 1970s) that strongly affirm lay ministry in the world, but one finds relatively few congregations giving deliberate, sustained attention to this aspect of the Christian mission. Among most people, when "ministry of the laity" is discussed with conviction, the conversation tends to focus more on laypeople's volunteer roles within the church than on their everyday roles within the secular world (a fact driven partly by increased financial pressures within the churches, partly by an expansion of congregation-based activities, and partly by a dwindling supply of clergy).

Episcopal clergyman Loren Mead well describes the anomalous situation among the American churches:

> "Ministry of the laity" is a cliché today, so routine that it's almost boring. Nobody questions it . . . . It is also true that very few people seem to have much grasp of it and very little is consciously done about it in the denominations—other than talk about how important and good it is. For these and other reasons, it is hard today to recognize the revolutionary meaning in the phrase.[7]

Revisiting the Fundamentals

B ut the critical fact today is the presence of a small and growing minority gripped by the vision of Christians living their faith actively in the world of work. They are determined to recover and unleash the "revolutionary meaning" of this vision throughout the church, so that it is widely embraced and implemented among Christian people. They know it has such meaning and potential because it reflects fundamental truths of the gospel. These fundamentals not only challenge long-held views and practices but also provide the wellspring for what can become a reinvigorated Christianity.

This vision encompasses four central affirmations:

1. God's mission embraces the workplace.

When Jesus taught his disciples to pray "Thy kingdom come, Thy will be done on earth as it is in heaven" (Matthew 6:10), he was voicing a central conviction of biblical religion: God's gracious reign and redemptive mission reach to the whole world God has created and to every realm of every person's life.

God cares about workplaces because no part of the world's life has a greater impact—for good or ill, advancing or hindering God's mission—than the decisions made and the dramas acted out in countless workplaces around the globe.

Moreover, God cares about what happens in workplaces because God cares about the individual people who spend a large portion of their lives at work and are shaped significantly by what happens there.

God has a goal for every person. Each of us has been created in the divine image and is intended by God for a future, beginning now and extending beyond this present life, in which we and the whole creation are blessed by God's Spirit, are filled with perfect love, peace, and joy, and are brought into lasting communion with God.

This vision of God's future recurs throughout the Scriptures and is called by a variety of names ("the kingdom" and "the new creation" are the two we shall chiefly use). In the places and times when people's Christ-like acts accomplish God's will "on earth as it is in heaven," that experience gives them glimpses and foretastes of the kingdom, preparing them for God's intended future for them. But when people's experiences turn their affections and commitments in other directions, they resist God's will and frustrate God's intention for them.

Because of the importance of the workplace in shaping the world's future and people's lives, God is present in each workplace, seeking to awaken people to the blessed life of the kingdom, and to attract them to the paths leading toward it.

2. *The time has come for the church's mission to embrace the workplace.*

God calls the Christian community to be the chief instrument of the divine mission in the world. As one New Testament author puts it, "You are a chosen race, a royal priesthood, a holy nation, God's own people, that you may declare the wonderful deeds of him who called you out of darkness into his marvelous light" (1 Peter 2:9).

Because Christians already are present in workplaces virtually everywhere in the nation and because what happens there so greatly affects the lives of people—whether it is the classroom, the fire station, the Oval Office, or the second shift at the deli—this mission frontier has a priority claim upon the church. Here the gospel's "marvelous light" must be affirmed and demonstrated by Christian laypeople. Here they must act in ways that allow its life-healing and life-transforming power to make a difference.

In our own time, as the church discovers this neglected dimension of its mission, it will find itself visited afresh by

God's Spirit, who works to energize the whole church and each Christian for participation in God's mission in the world.

And, as some observers have noted, when pastors and other church leaders catch this vision and give proper attention to helping laypeople address tough issues of daily life and work, they will find that the church wins the active participation and financial support of men and women who presently are disenchanted with this institution that helps them so little with everyday issues that matter to them so much.[8]

3. Taking faith to work brings spiritual renewal to Christians.

Each of us who prays for the coming of God's kingdom most fully experiences its peace and power when we offer ourselves, like Jesus, to be used by God as instruments through whom others can know the demands and joys of the kingdom.

God calls us to make this self-offering and to receive the Spirit's empowerment in every realm of our lives, not just in the workplace. When those of us who work make this self-offering in the workplace, where such practice typically is difficult and elusive, we discover God's presence there. It is experienced as a gracious power moving us beyond our hesitations and enabling us to live the gospel and to manifest something of God's blessed future.

We then are empowered to become means, albeit imperfect ones, for helping others in the workplace catch glimpses of God's new creation and journey on their own paths toward that destination. At such times, "the power at work within us" does indeed accomplish "far more . . . than all that we ask or think" (Ephesians 3:20).

To the degree that this happens, our life in the workplace takes on new purposefulness and satisfaction. We know that even if parts of our work experience continue to be disagreeable, something extraordinary is happening. Our workplace is becoming a place of grace and we are being blessed there.

4. *Discipleship at work brings health and vitality to secular institutions.*

At a time when many workplaces and institutions are dispirited and stressed, attached to values and patterns of institutional life that encourage unethical and uncaring behavior, those workplaces need an infusion of a power capable of making them more humane and more productive. And for the many people who know how barren their work has become and are eager to find meaning in it, the time is ripe for the discovery of a spiritual fountainhead capable of making work purposive and satisfying.

The millions of Christians present in workplaces in this country and around the world constitute an enormous, but as yet barely tapped, source of fresh vitality for a multitude of institutions and, through them, for the whole human family. As the Gospel of Matthew says, reflecting ancient civilization's experience of the life-enhancing quality of salt, Jesus' disciples are "the salt of the earth." It is difficult to imagine something happening with more far-reaching beneficial consequences than for present-day Christians to discover and exercise their "saltness."

So, at the start of a new century and millennium, the stage is set for Christian people to recognize and embrace the role God intends for them in the workplace. As that happens, the twenty-first century truly will become a time of new beginnings.

What exactly is that role?

A Pioneer's Story

One of the most notable advances ever made in Christians' thinking about workplace ministry was set forth in 1991, by an American Lutheran layman, William E. Diehl (pronounced "deal"). Before that time, most discussion about serving God in the workplace remained at the level of generalities. Diehl now proposed a practical model of everyday ministry that was relevant to every Christian who works. This breakthrough came after Diehl's long personal journey of spiritual discovery and an ever-deepening understanding of lay ministry. His story deserves telling.

As a young man, William Diehl was like many other Christian laypeople in the 1950s, active in his congregation, but receiving little help there in thinking about the actual difference his faith could make at work. Looking back on those years, Diehl later said: "My Sunday experience had no connection to my Monday world. The words that came to me from the Bible and the pulpit made no sense to me in my weekday world."

To his dismay, Diehl realized that many people in his congregation welcomed the separation. They were eager for a break from the pressures and problems of the workplace. Moreover, his congregation gave tacit approval to the Sunday-Monday disconnect by encouraging members to think they fulfilled their lay ministry responsibilities through volunteering for important church-centered tasks and by contributing their hard-earned funds to the church. In Diehl's case, his teaching of a Sunday school class and serving on the church council led to his winning an award for being an exemplary layperson.

But he knew that as useful as such deeds might be, something was missing. As a good Lutheran, he had absorbed

Martin Luther's sixteenth-century discovery that God calls all the baptized, not just monks and clergy, to participate in Christ's priesthood. More critically, by the late 1950s Diehl had begun to read books by European and North American church leaders caught up in the momentous discovery of God's summons to ministry in the workplaces of the world.

In this period of creative discontent, William Diehl was looking for a way of understanding the difference his faith could make to the tough issues he encountered day after day in his sales (and later, managerial) job at Bethlehem Steel. What should he do about the friend working for another company who wanted a "special consideration" in their business transaction? About the likable subordinate who was doing shoddy work? About the colleague who was pushing her religion on employees? About mounting pressures from environmentalists? About his own opportunity for advancement at the cost of more time away from his family?

The spiritual journey Diehl embarked upon has been described in his eight books written between 1970 and 2003. None of them has made a larger mark than *The Monday Connection*, published in 1991.[9] Diehl's presentation there of a practical model for every Christian's ministry in daily life has the merit both of taking into account all areas of a person's work experience and of including all the outreach responsibilities to which God invites Christians involved in the world of work. It provides valuable conceptual tools and guidelines for helping a person think concretely about opportunities for ministry present in the daily routines of the workplace. And it provides an antidote for any Christians tempted to think their work is unchallenging or unimportant.

My own reflection on Diehl's model of workplace ministry has led me to make a few shifts in its presentation and theological accents, so as to make it fit better with my own experience and understanding. I encourage readers to make comparable amendments in my restatement of the model, if doing so helps them embrace it and put it into practice.

Overview of Christians'
Four-Part Ministry at Work

As I understand God's intention for Christians in the workplace, we are summoned to make our work a part of God's work for the coming of the kingdom. We do so through:

A *ministry of competence:* serving God and neighbor by doing our work well, through full use of the gifts God has given each of us, so that the human family is built up and moved nearer the abundant life of the kingdom.

A *ministry of caring:* being attentive and responsive to the needs and hurts of people in our workplace, so that they experience something of the authentic community God intends for the human family.

A *ministry of ethics:* moving perceptions and practices of right and wrong at work to a higher level, so that workplace ethics better approximate the ways God wills people to live together.

A *ministry of change:* developing new institutional practices and systems that help all people be and do their best, so that the place of work more nearly becomes a place of grace.

In the next two chapters this four-part model of workplace ministry will be examined closely. I believe that with practice and persistence, many Christians will be able to carry it out in each job they hold, though probably not all four parts with equal intensity or effect. But there are some jobs and circumstances where one or perhaps even several parts will be out of reach. Blessed is the person in a job and circumstances where action occurs on all four fronts.

Two important questions are raised by this way of viewing Christians' workplace ministry:

1. *Will such activity, joined with Christians' other ministries in the world, result in the consummation of God's kingdom?* No. The kingdom belongs to God, and it is God who determines when the kingdom will come in its fullness and how much of our earthly accomplishments will be embraced by it. Meanwhile, sin and evil continue to resist God's intentions and to damage people. Our vocation is to witness to the new life of the kingdom in all we say and do, in the workplace and in every realm of life. We do so confident that God will make use of our words and deeds to prepare us and others for God's gracious future.

2. *Is there a place for evangelism in Christians' workplace ministry?* Yes. Witness to the good news of God's kingdom is a task to which God calls us in every realm of life. It pervades all four parts of our ministry at work. It is also a witness to Jesus Christ, for he is the one in whom the kingdom is present most fully and seen most clearly. We can hope that people in the workplace are so struck by our deeds that they ask why we do them. We then should seek appropriate ways to tell them it is because of what we have learned about the meaning of life from Jesus Christ. Meanwhile, our daily witness-by-deeds to kingdom life can help confirm people's deep hunger for a better future and give them a glimpse of what God has in mind for the human family.

Someone has aptly said that most people in workplaces today do not regularly read Matthew,

Mark, Luke, or John. But they do see us, day after day. Our calling is to be for them "the fifth Gospel."

We now must look more closely at Christians' ministries of competence, caring, ethics, and change.

Chapter Two

Making a Difference in the Workplace

Making a Difference
in the Workplace

"It is a gross error to suppose that the Christian cause goes forward solely or chiefly on weekends. What happens on the regular weekdays may be far more important, so far as the Christian faith is concerned, than what happens on Sunday . . . . The idea is that God can call us to many kinds of activity and that secular work well done is a holy enterprise."
Elton Trueblood, 1952[10]

In this chapter we shall address two ways that Christians can take faith to work "on the regular weekdays" and make an impact there: the *ministry of competence* and the *ministry of caring*.

Before examining these issues directly, we must note a fundamental theme that will run through our entire discussion of Christians' workplace ministry. Any serious consideration of the church's mission in the world must confront a set of questions that have occupied Christians since the earliest years of Christianity. How do Christ and culture, the gospel and the world, the kingdom and secular society properly relate to each other? Should Christians affirm culture, the world, and secular society, or should we oppose them? Or, should we undertake some measure of both affirmation and opposition? What does it mean, as the seventeenth chapter of the Gospel of John counsels, to be *in* the world but not *of* the world?

Assessing Workplace Values

My own understanding of biblical faith leads me to believe that faithful following of Christ at work requires that we declare both a "Yes" and a "No" to people and values we interact with in the workplace. Our "Yes" is directed to what is good in the workplace. We affirm those things gratefully, and we recognize God's hand in them. We do so because the Creator has endowed the human family with great worth and enormous capacity for good (as befits those called to be God's partners). Other religious and humanistic traditions also constitute a potent source of positive values. Persons guided by those traditions often can be Christians' allies in the quest for workplaces more attuned to God's intentions for the human family.

Our "No" is directed to what is amiss in the workplace, to practices and patterns that conflict with God's new creation. We know that certain of the strongest values in many workplaces today are negative ones. One way to identify those values is to note the "isms" that observers of our modern-day workplace culture have coined as descriptors. They speak, for example, of the presence of *materialism, consumerism, careerism, ageism,* and *workaholism* (in addition to the *racism* and *sexism* that have a long history in American life). Another way is to state the maxims, the alleged "truths," one frequently hears in the world of work. Hence:

> *What really matters is the bottom line.*
> *We (I) will do whatever it takes to get ahead.*
> *It's a dog-eat-dog world.*
> *Above all, look out for Number One.*

(list continued on next page)

Business is business.
The bigger (the more), the better.
Don't rock the boat.
Everybody does it.
Nobody will notice.

The power of these negative values (that are akin to what some New Testament authors call "principalities and powers"[11]) is not confined to the workplace. They are expansive, seeking a foothold in other realms of life as well. Consequently, we can find ourselves tempted to allow our homes, our leisure, and even our religious institutions to fall under their control.

Clearly, Christians engaged in workplace ministry need the courage and the creativity to stand against these negative values. We not only must resist their expansion but also seek to replace them in the workplace with values that reflect the abundant life of God's new creation.

As we do so, it is important to recognize that a growing quest for new, positive values is already present in many workplaces. People today are seeking patterns of leadership and relationship that are more humane and life-affirming than the ones that have long prevailed. Several decades ago, Studs Terkel reported that his extensive study of American working people's experience and attitudes found that they increasingly view their work as being "about daily meaning as well as daily bread." They are looking, he said, for "recognition as well as cash . . . in short for a sort of life rather than a Monday through Friday sort of dying."[12]

Since Terkel's study, people's eagerness for a discovery of "daily meaning" at their work has become intense. It often is accompanied by pursuit of "spirituality" in the workplace. That term is understood differently by people, but among many it bespeaks a hunger for a "higher power" capable of giving human life a deeper grounding than any that our secular culture provides. Often the church experiences of such "seekers" have made them wary of institutional religion. If, however, churches can provide a hospitable, affirming environment to these people, they may yet become significant participants in the churches' workplace mission.[13]

Four Instructive Voices

Four American Christians long engaged in workplace ministry have faced the challenge of negative workplace values creatively and have written helpfully about their experiences. Chris Satullo, who for thirteen years was managing editor of *The Express*, a Pennsylvania newspaper, testifies to the "huge daily struggle" the Christian undertakes in combating dominant workplace values. "Make no mistake—the workplace is this nation's great unrecognized church; each workplace, each profession has its own culture, its own set of values. They are largely unexamined, but they are relentlessly inculcated, relentlessly enforced." In his own newspaper culture Satullo acknowledges the presence of a cynicism often at odds with gospel values. But he also affirms that with the grace of God and the support of a faith community, slow progress can be made in the struggle. "Each day we must examine the religion of our workplace and nudge it a little closer toward the gospel, at least in the way we work, if not in the way our colleagues do."[14]

Max De Pree, CEO for many years of Herman Miller, Inc., a Michigan-based Fortune 500 manufacturer of office furniture, also knows the power of secular values. A major problem for Christians, he says, is the temptation to accept the mindset prevailing in the institutions where we work. "It happens without thinking about it. Unless somebody articulates something different, you are going to adopt a secular standpoint without even thinking about it." De Pree has led the way in articulating "something different." A key for him is deliberately integrating all aspects of one's life around core values that endure. For De Pree, this integration is based upon values rooted in Christian faith, not upon those of the workplace: "We integrate our work up to the level of our faith."[15]

Sandra Herron, former Vice President and Manager of Sales and Service at Bank One in Indianapolis, considers the Christian's tasks of workplace ministry as a continuation of Christ's prophetic, kingly, and priestly roles. A principal part of this effort must be to "challenge the status quo and envision a new reality that brings us closer to the values of the kingdom." Herron stresses the importance, when undertaking this challenge, of offering a concrete, practicable alternative to established routine—by proposing, for example, in place of the traditional employee incentive plan, a new one that "encourages teamwork and provides for a more equitable distribution of rewards."[16]

Tom Chappell, founder and CEO of Tom's of Maine, a manufacturer of natural personal care products, tells of his struggle on the values front. At a time when he was eager to expand his business, he yielded to pressures to let the company be controlled by such standard corporate values as making profit maximization supreme and regarding customers and employees as mere numbers. But, eventually, he dug in his heels. He renewed his determination to demonstrate that a firm which governs itself by higher values and embraces sound business processes can succeed in the fiercely competitive world of commerce. This, Chappell believes, is the way to a "new kind of capitalism," where business firms learn to "do well by doing good."[17]

As executives, Chris Satullo, Max De Pree, Sandra Herron, and Tom Chappell have held sufficient authority in their hands that they could initiate actions aimed at dethroning some of the "false gods" of their work cultures. Most of us are not in such positions. We have a less sweeping range of influence. But it is critical to remember that each of us does have a circle of influence. It may be small—perhaps no more than one's own soul. There we can take a stand for kingdom values.

Each of the four parts of workplace ministry (see page 25) provides an opportunity for us to take such a stand and become participants in God's mission in the world.

 ## The Ministry of Competence

Serving God and neighbor by doing our work well, through full use of the gifts God has given each of us, so that the human family is built up and moved nearer the abundant life of the kingdom.

A fundamental feature of the *ministry of competence* is suggested by a statement Martin Luther King, Jr. once made to a group: "If it falls to your lot to be a street sweeper, sweep streets like Michelangelo carved marble. Sweep streets as Shakespeare wrote pictures. Sweep streets so well that all the hosts of heaven will have to say, 'Here lies the street sweeper who did his job well.'"[18]

King makes a point crucial to Christian discipleship and to our workplace ministry: God wants us to take our work seriously, to give it our best effort, so that we do it well. Why is this so? Because we who follow Christ are called to be God's partners in the great task of making the divine creation a blessing to all who occupy the earth with us. This is the meaning of God's commission to Adam in the Garden of Eden to "till it and keep it" (Genesis 2:15). Consequently, when we do the work of providing goods and services to meet human needs, we do it not just for our customers, our clients, our patients, our students, our colleagues, our bosses, or our families. Most fundamentally, we do it for God. This is the truth running throughout Scripture and captured pointedly in the words of Colossians 3:23: "Whatever your task, work heartedly, as serving the Lord and not men."

Especially critical for understanding the ministry of competence is biblical authors' teaching about "charisms." They affirm that God gives each of us certain gifts (charisms) to be used in serving each other and thus contributing to the fulfillment of God's purposes for the church and the world. In 1 Corinthians 12:4-7, Paul writes: "There are varieties of gifts but the same Spirit. There are varieties of service, but the same Lord . . . . In each of us the Spirit is manifested in one particular way, for some useful purpose" (New English Bible). The same point occurs with a different accent in 1 Peter 4:10: "Like good stewards of the manifold grace of God, serve one another with whatever gift each of you has received" (NRSV).

When we look at our workplaces in light of God's having gifted people "for some useful purpose," to "serve one another," we quickly recognize that our work world, in fact, is often controlled by other purposes. As a result, some workplaces make work dull and spiritless; some cause it to demand too much from people and grind them down. Either way there is often too little joy in work and too little incentive to be and do our best there.

Implications for Us

When we Christians consider our work lives from the perspective of biblical teaching about gifts, important questions press themselves upon each of us. Younger people looking toward their future work must ask: What are the gifts God has bestowed on me, and where can I use them in ways that not only allow me to earn an income adequate to meet my family responsibilities, but also to serve God's purposes in the world? Those Christians already in the workforce must ask: Am I in the line of work (and in the particular job) where, along with earning an adequate income, my gifts are being put to productive use for God? If I suspect I am not, and I see no realistic prospect for change at present, when and how can I make a change? If I must wait indefinitely for change to become a real option, how can I live constructively with this fact, without turning bitter or complacent in the process?

Debbie Price is a person who struggled with questions of vocational discernment. She was working as an interior designer in Colorado when she grew restless and recognized she must make a change. Here is what she later wrote:

> I finally . . . realized I wasn't being valuable to anyone. Nor was I able to be enthusiastic about any aspect of my work. I also realized that it wasn't right for me to be doing what the job required. Not that there was anything dishonest or illegal involved, but I was being paid on a commission basis—30 percent of the gross profit. One client spent twenty thousand dollars on furnishings for a 10 x 12 room. I began to question my motivation for encouraging people to buy—I really couldn't believe that it was good stewardship of my

talents to be persuading customers to spend huge sums of money on furniture.

As Price looked at her options, she realized that "you should consider what the job is asking you to do . . . . Is the result of your labor truly worthwhile, serving the community and honoring God?" Realizing it was not and embarking on a career move, she first became an administrative assistant and education director at a Baptist church, and later she moved on to become scheduling secretary for a United States senator.[19]

But becoming more aware of one's God-given vocation in the workplace does not necessarily lead to a job change. During a period of vocational re-examination, John Zeller, an accountant, initially suspected that his wife's work as a nurse was more in line with what God intended for him. After all, it clearly was an opportunity for service to others, and it brought frequent, often poignant, rewards. But, upon prayerful reflection and in conversation with people who knew him well (the key ways that most Christians discern God's call), Zeller realized that being a "numbers cruncher" was the direction his aptitude, strengths, and experience took him. Also, he came to recognize that his work had an important beneficial effect. "Now, . . . I appreciate that I directly impact the 80 people who work for my company. My work is meaningful if I can use my God-given gifts to do the best possible job and to keep my fellow employees at their jobs."[20]

We especially need to think about the implications of this perspective regarding vocation for those Christians who are at either the earlier or the later stages of life's journey. In our culture today, young people are bombarded by countless messages about career and job; few of those messages encourage them to make their decisions about work in light of a biblical perspective. Just how secularized this critical decision has become is suggested by a recent national survey. It found that only 22% of people who attend church weekly had chosen their work with any attention at all to what their faith teaches about work. Well might we begin to ponder: What can Christian parents and congregations do to help our children make career and job choices within a framework of meaning provided by biblical faith?[21]

American culture also sends frequent signals to older people about the self-indulgent ways they should spend their retirement years. With seniors living longer and with increasing requests for volunteers in places where human needs are being addressed, churches must challenge their older members' thinking: How will you now use your talents in service to God and neighbor?

Such questions about faith, work, and vocation must be given a higher priority on the churches' agenda. We need to struggle with them as individuals, and in our congregations we need to learn how to help each other in the struggle.

Meanwhile, those of us engaged in work we believe is being performed competently, because it is a fruitful use of our God-given talents, should be deeply grateful for this privilege. Such persons are on the way to fulfilling Richard Bolles' wise admonition, "Exercise the Talent which you particularly came to Earth to use . . . in those place(s) or setting(s) which God has caused to appeal to you most, and for those purposes which God most needs to have done in the world."[22] People with this kind of commitment and joy in their work are a powerful leaven in the workplace. They perhaps exemplify what an Old Testament author had in mind: "It is God's gift that every one should . . . . take pleasure in all their toil" (Ecclesiastes 3:13 NRSV).

But what about those of us who are now stuck in a job we do not enjoy and know does not engage our God-given gifts? Such persons should be on the lookout for other workplace doors that may yet open. And they should be grateful that God gives Christians ways beside the ministry of competence to take faith to work.

The Ministry of Caring

*B*eing attentive and responsive to the needs and hurts of people in our workplace, so that they experience something of the authentic community God intends for the human family.

Another of the ways we serve God's purposes for the workplace is the *ministry of caring*. This is the part of workplace witness we probably most naturally think of as a ministry or form of service (the Greek word *diakonia* can be translated by either of the two English words). The ministry of caring is our way of being sensitive to the people we interact with daily in the workplace. As uninteresting and unattractive as they sometimes may seem, the gospel prompts us to acknowledge them as neighbors given us by God to love. They are persons of great value, for God has created and endowed them; Christ has lived, died, and been resurrected for them; and God's Spirit now seeks their hearts and minds.

We may well discover that our ministry of caring wins the appreciation of co-workers, for most workplaces are filled with people eager for kind words and compassionate deeds. Such words and deeds often come like rain in a parched dessert.

But it is also true that we and our co-workers can be so focused on our work roles, and so eager to project an image of strength and self-sufficiency, that we discourage the flow of kindness and compassion in the workplace. When this happens, it is important to see beyond the masks, to remember that each worker has not only a divinely-bestowed value but also a human identity more fundamental than the workplace identity. We are daughters and sons, wives and husbands, sisters and brothers, who inevitably bring the joys and pains, the emotional highs and lows of those relationships with us to work. The quality of our work is affected by the quality of those relationships, just as what happens at work will affect what happens at home. So, when we infuse a measure of human kindness into our interactions with people at work, who can say how far the ripples will reach?

Our work, says Max De Pree, "should and can be productive and rewarding, meaningful and maturing, enriching and fulfilling, healing and joyful." A key to elevating work environments to such a level, adds De Pree, is to make them places where people's potential as human beings is unlocked and nurtured. Such personal growth, in turn, is best fostered by workplace leaders and colleagues who take pains to create and maintain a caring work setting. "There are bags of research findings," notes British social philosopher Charles Handy, "to show that if you treat people as flowers they blossom, but if you think of them as weeds they shrink."[23]

The Bible abounds in pertinent words about the kind of caring that regards people as flowers rather than weeds. None say it better than 1 Corinthians 13:4-7. We do not often think about St. Paul's epistle as applying to our discipleship in the workplace. But we should:

> Love is patient and kind; love is not jealous or boastful; it is not arrogant or rude. Love does not insist on its own way; it is not irritable or resentful; it does not rejoice at wrong, but rejoices in the right. Love bears all things, believes all things, hopes all things, endures all things.

Such biblical descriptions of the work of love are not intended as lofty preachment for consumption only on Sunday. They affirm the lifestyle God intends for the kingdom and for those people empowered by God everyday to make their lives signposts pointing to the kingdom. The challenge to Christians is to seek the actualization, insofar as possible, of this vision of

God's future in the daily routines and relationships of life in the workplace.

As this happens, the ministry of caring will have a wide range of consequences, including the one especially important for organizations today of helping to generate a greater degree of respect, trust, and cooperation at work—qualities increasingly recognized as critical to workplace and organizational effectiveness.

Inevitably, people in different work environments will express Christian love in different ways. Here are brief glimpses of how the ministry of caring has been implemented in the lives of five Christians.

 ## Caring Demonstrated

For CEO Tom Chappell in Maine, the ministry of caring has meant building a corporate culture in his firm where employees are viewed (and view each other) as valued members of what he calls "a kind of extended family." Employees care about each other and enjoy working together in pursuit of the business values and objectives to which they feel personally committed. Generous provisions have been established for insurance benefits, child care, elder care, flextime, parental leave for birth and adoption (for both parents), and a compressed four-day work week for production employees. Reports Chappell: "We encourage our workers not to work late or on weekends, but to go home and enjoy themselves and their families." Such policies, Chappell adds, engender a high degree of employee loyalty to the firm, which he knows is a substantial business asset.[24]

Maxine Dennis is a cashier at a supermarket in Rhode Island. On the surface this appears to be a job offering few possibilities for Christian ministry. But Maxine Dennis does not live on the surface. "Compassion," she says, "is the most vital tool of my trade." She explains:

> There are many sad stories to be heard while ringing up grocery orders. Many times I find I'm called upon to help nurture the emotional state of shoppers— just as the food they're buying will provide nourishment to their bodies. Hearing of death, terminal illness, fatal accidents, and broken homes is all part of my job. During such times I try my utmost to listen with my heart, not just my ears. Often a single word of understanding or a mere look of genuine concern is just the right dose of medicine to help heal a bruised heart.[25]

John Finn, an environmental engineer in Massachusetts working with hazardous waste dumps, reminds us that the ministry of caring does not stop with our contemporaries or with the human community. It reaches out as well to future generations and to the natural environment. For Finn it involves probing for the truth beyond polluters' denials and obfuscations: "The sin had to be revealed before that small part of the earth could be healed." It also means bearing the frustration that comes with recognition of how little one person can do to address this vast problem. But John Finn persists in his determination to do all he can, knowing his work is part of a larger picture. "Compassion demands action. I most clearly see my work as ministry when I can help bring healing to those festering wounds which threaten the soil, water, and air that make life possible."[26]

Cecilia Newbold is a registered nurse seeking another kind of healing in a Colorado hospital. Her way of caring for comatose patients is a reminder of the lengths to which love will go. She writes:

> I have always felt that a comatose patient is much more aware of what is said and done in his or her presence than has been believed in the past. I talk to my unconscious patients. I greet them when I come into their rooms, tell them my name, and express aloud the hope that I can serve to make them more comfortable and to regain their health. When I turn a patient for nursing procedures, treatment, or medication, I say what I'm going to do, that there may be some discomfort, but that this procedure will help to make him or her more comfortable or aid in the recovery.[27]

Mary Elizabeth Dunne is an administrative law judge in New York who looks for ways to infuse a loving spirit into the bureaucratic processes she oversees. She tells of sitting at the table with a distraught woman who was seeking legal redress in a difficult case about compensation. When the woman began to cry, Judge Dunne performed a simple act of caring: "I reached out and took her hand. She calmed down, and I went on to the other 68 cases I had that day." Later she learned the woman had been so heartened by Dunne's kindness that she took initiatives which eventually helped get the case resolved in her favor.[28]

Christians' ministry of caring does not always lead to happy endings. Nor can we count on being able to watch all the ripples we have generated reach faraway shores. Sometimes such rewards come, but often they do not, and our ministry of caring can not be dependent upon them. It is rooted deeper, in the recognition that we are given the extraordinary privilege of being vessels through whom Christ's own ministry in the world continues. No one has made the point more memorably than St. Teresa of Avila:

Christ has no body on earth but yours, no hands but yours, no feet but yours; yours are the eyes through which Christ looks out in compassion to the world, yours are the feet with which he is to go about doing good, and yours are the hands with which he is to bless us now.[29]

Chapter Three

Helping the Place of Work Become a Place of Grace

Helping the Place of Work Become a Place of Grace

"Let the Christian who listens to the Word of the living God, uniting work with prayer, know the place his work has not only in earthly progress but also in the development of the kingdom of God . . . ."
Pope John Paul II, 1981[30]

As we Christians practice our faith at work, we must look for ways to plant the leaven of the gospel in every part of our work environments, so that its impact can reach as widely and deeply as possible. We thus contribute to the "development of the kingdom of God."

The model of a four-part workplace ministry (see page 25) is intended to help us find ways, some immediate and some long-term, to become creative bearers of the gospel and agents of the kingdom.

An important fact about the model of a four-part workplace ministry is that the four thrusts of this ministry are interrelated, connected to each other in a variety of ways. For example, a ministry of caring at times will push toward competence in one's response to a co-worker. If I am in a workplace situation where I find people eager for "someone who will just listen," this recognition prompts me to increase my listening skills, so that I can better carry out my ministry of caring. In this case, such growth in competence may come through as simple an act as talking with an experienced counselor or reading a good book on the topic, or it may require more. (See Chapter Two for discussion of the ministry of competence and the ministry of caring.)

As we turn our attention to the principal topics of this chapter—the ministry of ethics and the ministry of change—we must recognize that considerable interplay exists between these two expressions of the Christian's workplace responsibility. In exercising the ministry of change, for example, an important task is to look for ways that people's work environments can be improved so as to decrease the negative influences pushing them toward unethical action and to increase the positive influences pushing them toward ethical action. And, we must employ ethical means of effecting workplace change, lest we stumble into unethical means that foul rather than cleanse the work environment.

The Ministry of Ethics

*M*oving perceptions and practices of right and wrong at work to a higher level, so that workplace ethics better approximate the ways God wills people to live together.*

Our consideration of the *ministry of ethics* comes at a time when many Americans are concerned about the decline in both public and private morality (note that I am using the terms "morality" and "ethics" interchangeably). Numerous studies have tracked this development. An extensive 1991 nationwide survey, for example, concluded that "a letdown in moral values is now considered the number one problem facing our country." Nine years later a widely read study reported that two-thirds of Americans think that "social and moral values" have declined.[31] People differ widely in their diagnosis of this problem, as well as in their prescription of remedies. But it seems clear that in our rapidly changing, more heterogeneous society, for many people today "distinguishing between right and wrong" and "choosing of right over wrong" have each become highly problematic matters.

But there are also encouraging signs. A key one is acknowledgment by an increasing number of leaders that their institutions' long-term success is tied to our society's recognizing and heeding the moral infrastructure that underpins all human interaction. They know that institutions of every kind function better in the long run when people act honestly, for example, than when they act dishonestly. Some institutional leaders are acknowledging, as well, that they must take steps to preserve and strengthen the commitments and habits constituting this moral infrastructure. Prominent among these steps is the launching of programs to formulate and implement codes of ethical conduct. Initiatives of this kind can be observed most notably in the business world, but they also exist in such diverse circles as the armed forces, government agencies, professional associations, and educational institutions.

Churches also appear to be recognizing that they must do more to shed gospel light on the kinds of ethical issues arising in the workplace. For much of the twentieth century, the churches' ethical attention was so captured by a succession of urgent, headline-making issues (often related to war and peace, at times also to macro-economic and racial themes) that the commonplace issues arising in the ordinary routines of work life were slighted. This has resulted in what theologian Miroslav Volf calls a "dire deficiency in Protestant social ethics" (a comparable statement could be made about Catholic social ethics). But this deficiency is beginning to be addressed, and the building of an up-to-date store of pertinent ethical wisdom for Christians in the workplace deserves a prominent place on the churches' long-term ethics agenda.[32]

Christians who become engaged in this task need to be aware of the important strides made in recent decades by scholars addressing ethics issues in such secular disciplines as Organizational Behavior and Business Ethics. We do well also to recognize the steps taken by a host of secular institutions to strengthen the ethical fabric of their organizational life and to promote ethical behavior in the workplace. In those quarters Christians often will find insight that illumines the values of God's kingdom; for this they should give thanks for God's continued teaching and nurturing of the human family. But Christians also will find points at which this effort has fallen short; in such cases Christians must enter into dialogue with secular colleagues so as to bear informed witness to what they know of God's will for how people should conduct themselves. For example: Many secular proponents of ethical behavior in the workplace need to be reminded that compliance with an organization's ethics code, while preferable to non-compliance, is not nearly so desirable as encouraging in a person the commitment to avoid evil and do good, as well as nurturing the underlying character and organizational environment that will sustain such commitment and conduct over the long haul.

Persons concerned about the bearing of ethics upon the world of work, whether operating from a religious or a secular perspective, must recognize too that ethical choices frequently are made in complex, ambiguous situations colored by shades of gray. Corporate executive James Autry describes a fact of work life experienced by many ethically concerned people both within and beyond the business realm:

> We rarely get the easy choices—wrong versus right, good versus evil—that seem so apparent to those who are not engaged in management every day. Too often the choices are between the better of two "rights" or the lesser of two "wrongs." This is true whether the choice involves the rights and needs of one member of the group versus the rights and needs of the group as a whole, or the "right price" to a customer versus the

"right return" on the owner's investment. This is to say nothing of the increasing pressures of environmental concerns, safety concerns, hiring practices, advertising claims, and on and on.[33]

What then is the Christian ministry of ethics in the workplace today? What ethical consequences follow from our commitment to follow Christ at work and become advocates there for the ways of God's kingdom?

 ## Seeking the High Road

Scripture and the Christian past constitute a rich reservoir of ethical wisdom for daily life, with a variety of approaches having been developed to understand our ethical responsibilities. One of the most persistent of these approaches has looked to biblical teaching about Jesus and the kingdom. A central theme within this teaching is a two-fold recognition. The first is that the Lord calls his followers to an extraordinarily high standard of behavior and purpose such as "Be perfect, therefore, as your heavenly Father is perfect (Matthew 5:48 NRSV)," and "Your kingdom come, Your will be done on earth as it is in heaven (Matthew 6:10 NRSV)." The second is that he knows we often will fail to reach this high level of character and conduct, and thus will need the grace and power of God in order to be forgiven and started anew on the journey of discipleship.

For Christians engaged in the workplace ministry of ethics, this means that we must be alert to opportunities to move our own behavior and that of our workplaces and institutions as close as possible to the high road of ethical conduct we find reflected in biblical teachings. Among these teachings are the Ten Commandments in Exodus 20, where within this ancient code we read "You shall not steal"; the Sermon on the Mount in Matthew 5, where Jesus' teachings include "Blessed are the merciful, for they shall obtain mercy"; and the Pauline epistles, where words like those of Romans 12:9 remind us of the way of life dawning in God's new creation—"Let love be genuine; hate what is evil, hold fast to what is good."

But as we seek to travel this road, we quickly discover how difficult the journey can be (usually more so for institutional than for individual conduct). At these times we need to engage our moral imagination to find patterns of behavior that approximate the intended route as closely as possible. When we fall short, we make our "responsible compromises" in the assurance that the forgiving God continues to embrace us and will empower us for ever-renewed efforts to reach the high road.

Christians experience this struggle in relation to numerous ethics issues present in the workplace. One of the most persistent and vexing is honesty—a traditional precept and virtue that is both widely extolled and frequently compromised. The Bible repeatedly affirms the importance of honesty, and experts in Organizational Behavior and Business Ethics recognize its indispensability for productive workplaces. Most modern-day Christian ethicists, however, have paid relatively little attention to its complexities and nuances.

Christians in the workplace who are eager to practice the ministry of ethics must repeatedly face the question of how honestly they will act and encourage others to act, especially when acting honestly is not consistent with other important considerations (including other values). For example: Will the secretary follow her boss's instruction to tell a caller (falsely) that he is not in? Will the salesperson repeat the sales manager's inflated claim for the product? Will the department chairperson share bad news about the department's future that almost certainly will lead the valued young instructor to accept a position in another university? Will the junior executive tell the senior executive that one of the latter's favorite plans for the future is seriously flawed? Will the candidate for office tell voters that the public schools cannot be rescued unless taxes are increased? Will the high school teacher give the student the grade his work deserves or the one that will help him win the scholarship?

These are not easy questions and they deserve more probing than they usually receive. Christians, standing in unique personal and workplace circumstances, will perhaps answer them in different ways. But no matter what their circumstances, Christians must attempt to act with thoroughgoing honesty in all such situations. That is partly because honesty is crucial for fostering trust, which in turn is indispensable for fostering open communication and vitality in organizations. More than that, because we are imitators of a loving God, we must recognize (as Lutheran ethicist James Childs has aptly said) that "truthfulness is an expression of love's concern for the well-being of those affected" by our words and deeds.[34]

We Christians must become more adept at thinking carefully and acting responsibly regarding a wide range of tough ethical questions arising at work, not just those where honesty is the focus. Doing so in concert with fellow Christians not only can throw useful light on our ethical quandaries, it also can identify a group of supportive friends who will stand with us when our workplace decisions cause us the discomfort, and possibly the jeopardy, of swimming against the tide. And it will model a pattern of graced ethical seriousness badly needed in institutions throughout our society.

Examples of Christians acting this way in the workplace are not difficult to find. Construction executive Jack Feldballe tells the story of a decision he faced in circumstances where his business responsibility and his Christian ethical responsibility initially pulled in opposite directions.

We were in the process of thinking about forming a new consulting firm with an employee of another firm that was in trouble for various financial reasons and was going to close its doors. Were we to create the new firm, it would have to have some clients. There was a client base at the old firm, and the old contracts with these clients had run out.

Using one of the best law firms in town, we determined that there was absolutely no legal obligation not to take on one of the old clients. You couldn't induce anyone to breach their old contract, but you could go after the client for new contracts.

The owners of the old firm didn't see it that way. Perhaps they believed they had rights. Perhaps they were posturing. Anyway, they wanted money. What should we do?

I stepped back and said, "I know what the legal obligation is, but what's the ethical obligation from my set of ethics?" I'm reminded that we're taught very clearly in Scripture that the fulfilling of the law is in part to treat others as you would want to be treated. So that becomes a standard.

So I said to myself, Wait a minute. If I were sitting on the other side, with great financial problems, I might feel I created and nurtured these clients over a couple of years.

I thought about this all that weekend, and on Monday morning we made an offer to share the profit with that individual (the former owner) for one year on these clients. She was ecstatic, and not only that, but she then got on the phone and helped us finalize a contract with that client, which was a large automotive company. And we got a contract out of it.[35]

Business ethicist Laura Nash, to whom Feldballe related this experience, has noted that at a critical moment in his thinking about the issue, Feldballe's faith led him to "apply Christian teachings to the little details," and he made an offer that went beyond the requirements of both the law and normal business practice. In this case there apparently was a happy outcome for all parties. Though there is ample evidence that such outcomes are by no means guaranteed to Christians who act ethically in the workplace, we must not let the cynical climate of our time blind us to the fact that, as Paul affirms in Romans 8:28, "We know that in everything God works for good with those who love him, who are called according to his purpose." This happens even in the workplace.

 ## The Ministry of Change

*D*eveloping *new institutional practices and systems that help all people be and do their best, so that the place of work more nearly becomes a place of grace.*

We turn next to consider the *ministry of change*. In considering this topic, it will be helpful to pursue first a point made at the beginning of the chapter. A principal reason for our effort to bring change to workplace environments is the responsibility to correct conditions pushing people to unethical actions, as well as the responsibility to create conditions encouraging them to take ethical actions. Observers of workplace behavior have noted, for example, that corporate codes of conduct calling for employee honesty are likely to have minimal impact until changes are made in those features of workplace cultures that discourage and even punish honesty (such as compensation and promotion policies that reward employees who "make the numbers" without regard for how they did so).

The point about the pertinence of change for encouraging ethical conduct can be extended to recognize that we also must seek to create conditions that will foster competent and caring work. In our workplace ministry of change, we are looking farther upstream than today's crisis; we are seeking proactively to build the climate, policies, and systems that over time will elicit people's optimal individual and collective effort. We are seeking to open channels at work for the continuing inflow of God's grace.

The opportunities for effecting such change are different for people at different places in the workplace. Generally, the higher one's position, the more numerous and obvious will be the opportunities. But it is also true that the decentralizing of authority in many organizations today appears to be creating more opportunities at lower levels for initiating change.

Earlier we noted the workplace ministry efforts of Christian executives Sandra Herron and Max De Pree (pages 33-34). Herron's observations about seeking improvements at her bank deserve further attention. She knows how difficult it can be to move individuals and organizations beyond their established ways. "My company is like most others," she notes. "People spend a lot of time looking after their own psychological needs, delivering monologues on their opinions, guarding their turf, comparing their progress to that of others, trying to elevate their own status, and criticizing those who are different." But she is aware also that the status quo can be effectively challenged by pursuing the fact that many workplace changes that better reflect God's intentions for human interaction are economically beneficial as well. Effective customer service, for example, has positive consequences for her bank's bottom line, and Sandra Herron knows that the bank's attention to customers will not be improved without deliberate, sustained effort to foster a greater measure of mutual caring among employees.[36]

Max De Pree's observations about bringing change at Herman Miller, Inc. also deserve further attention. They apply not just to his firm but to many, and not just to leaders at the top levels of an organization, but to people in a wide range of positions. According to De Pree, we must recognize that every person and every organization has potential for greater achievement than has been realized so far; hence the fundamental responsibility of leaders at any level of an organization is to seek the changes by which that potential is realized. But present also, says De Pree, is a tendency in every organization toward deterioration or "entropy," where vision and energy are lost, apathy and bureaucratization take over, and change becomes extraordinarily difficult.

De Pree's practice of leadership at Herman Miller deliberately sought to prevent such a downward spiral by creating a climate conducive to personal and institutional growth. An important component of this process was the performance reviews he conducted periodically among senior managers. The probing questions he asked suggest the spirit in which any ministry of change should be pursued:

- What do you want to do (to be)? What are you planning to do about it?
- What two things should we do to work toward being a great company?
- What should grace enable us to be?
- What are three signals of impending entropy you see...? What are you going to do about it?[37]

These questions reveal four features of De Pree's strategy of change: 1) It recognizes that others must be respected for what they can bring to the quest for institutional improvement. 2) It encourages a deliberate focusing of strategic vision and implementation. 3) It acknowledges that power beyond our reckoning and control ("grace") is operating for positive change. 4) It takes pre-emptive action against negative change.

 ## A Roving Leader

Max De Pree also is helpful in reminding workplace Christians who do not occupy high-level positions that they too can make significant contributions toward change. This is done through what De Pree calls "roving leadership." He explains that organizations must recognize the fact that besides needing "hierarchical leaders," they also need "roving leaders." These are the individuals at every level in the organization who recognize a problem, then step "out of the box" to direct people's energies toward addressing the problem. "Roving leaders," says De Pree, "are those indispensable people in our lives who are there when we need them. Roving leaders take charge, in varying degrees, in a lot of companies every day."[38]

Melinda is such a person. She works as a secretary in the engineering department of a Fortune 500 corporation in Ohio. A colleague, impressed by the ways Melinda affects her workplace, has written about the range of influence she has won:

> She has been given extraordinary opportunities to teach classes and to participate in training programs that are not normally available to secretarial staff. She has begun to coordinate her company's participation in a minority internship program, and she serves as an informal mentor to many other minority employees who are early in their careers with the company.

But perhaps more than anything she does, what is most noticeable about Melinda is her maturity, professionalism, and inner strength . . . . Many of her co-workers would attest that, . . . in an environment where idle gossip and whining are pervasive, they have never heard her say a mean-spirited or negative word about anyone. But she does assertively present her opinions and feelings in a way that demonstrates that she . . . is looking for ways to take the initiative to make things better . . . . Others are drawn to her leadership and companionship.

For Melinda, the opportunity to influence the company is a ministry given her by God. Her colleague explains:

One of the most interesting aspects of Melinda's approach to work is that she prays before each meeting in which she will participate or each class or discussion she leads so that "the angels" will prepare the way and make a path for anything that God would have her do in that setting. Melinda prays for courage to say the things that may need to be said but others may be reluctant to express, and she asks that God will actively use her to influence the meeting in a way that is healthy and reflective of God's will for that group and area.[39]

Melinda's exercise of "roving leadership" does not occur accidentally. It occurs because she has prepared herself for it, both professionally and spiritually, and because she consciously seeks opportunities to make things happen that improve the climate and practices of her workplace. Melinda—and people like her—take steps to help God's will be done on earth as it is in heaven.

Reshaping Work

The ways people understand and carry out their work roles have evolved greatly over the centuries, with some of the most far-reaching changes having occurred in the twentieth century. An important recent example has been the expansion in the number of hours typically spent at work. An especially critical part of this development is the involvement now of a high percentage of women in work outside the home.

There is still a sizable minority of Americans, however, who have not participated in our economy's expansion and barely make ends meet. Christians must be engaged in seeking the changes that will help these people win and keep a productive place in the workplace. And so, too, must changes be sought among the majority. For them increased work has often brought more consumer products and a higher standard of living—but at the cost of serious physical, psychological, and social problems. Economist Juliet Schor suggests the magnitude of that cost. Increased work, she says, is a major factor in the dramatic rise of stress and a variety of other unwelcome consequences.

> Stress-related diseases have exploded, especially among women, and jobs are a major factor . . . . Sleep has become another casualty of modern life. According to sleep researchers, studies point to a "sleep deficit" among Americans, a majority of whom are currently getting between 60 and 90 minutes less a night than they should for optimum health and performance . . . . The stress has placed tremendous burdens on marriages . . . . Serious as these problems are, the most alarming development may be the effect of the work explosion on the care of children. According to economist Sylvia

Hewlett, "child neglect has become endemic in our society." A major problem is that children are increasingly left alone, to fend for themselves while their parents are at work.[40]

It is not enough to lament such developments. Christians' ministry of change compels us to seek the sources of the problems and to contribute whatever measure of long-term transformation we can, especially to the ways work is understood and structured in our society today.

Regarding the understanding of work, philosopher Lee Hardy rightly affirms that Christians should steer "a middle path between the vilification and the glorification of work." There is no place for the kind of vilification that regards work as intrinsically degrading and thus as an activity to be shunned. To the contrary, work is an arena where people can use their gifts to contribute to the realization of God's purposes for the human family. But neither is there place for a glorification of work, which occurs when people hold inflated expectations for work and over-invest themselves in their workplace roles. A healthy antidote to such excess lies in recognizing that our work provides only one part of our identity and constitutes only one element in the totality of ways we respond to God's call. Says Hardy:

> After I've done my job as an employee, I still have other things to do as a spouse, a parent, a parishioner, a neighbor, and a citizen—not to mention the fact I am also called to rest in leisurely contentment with God's goodness on the Sabbath. If I pour myself into my work, with nothing left over to give my spouse, my children, church, community, or country, I have neither heard nor heeded the full scope of God's call in my life.[41]

This understanding of the important but limited role of work in human life has implications both for individuals and for organizations. For individuals it is a caution against an inordinate commitment to work, especially when that commitment is stoked by the desire to possess more and more of the "goods" prized by a consumerist society. We need constantly to hear the voices reminding us that "enough is enough," and that "it is more blessed to give than to receive."

But organizations also have a responsibility, especially in the way they design jobs. Pope John XXIII struck the right note by affirming that it is not enough for an economy or organization to excel at producing wealth and creating jobs. It matters greatly that the kind of jobs be created which will have the optimal formative influence upon the people holding them. "There is," the pope said, "an innate need of human nature requiring that . . . [people] engaged in productive activity have an opportunity to assume responsibility and perfect themselves by their efforts." Consequently, if jobs are structured in such a way that the "human dignity of workers is compromised, or their sense of responsibility is weakened, or their freedom of action is removed," a serious injustice has occurred.[42]

Lee Hardy concurs with this perspective and maintains that the contemporary management theories best embracing the gospel value of economic justice are those acknowledging that jobs should be designed so as to allow employees adequate time for important non-work pursuits. They also acknowledge that jobs should engage employees "as whole persons, as creatures with high-level capacities for thought, imagination, and responsible choice as well as motor abilities. Our jobs ought to be places where the whole person can respond to the call of God."[43]

A significant body of research shows that companies that have deliberately sought to design jobs in such people-affirming ways usually are recognized as superior places to work, their employees are more productive, and they enjoy success at the bottom line. Doing good and doing well frequently go hand-in-hand.

An instructive example of such a workplace is the law firm of Wheeler, Upham, Bryant and Uhl, located in Grand Rapids, Michigan. Its founders deliberately built the firm's culture to reflect Christian values. According to the corporate statement of purpose, one of the firm's principal values is "to recognize the importance of our employees' personal development, and their family, community, religious, and other like commitments unrelated to the practice of law." This respect for employees' lives is seen in several important policies: Fewer billable hours are expected of associates than is customary in law firms, secretaries rarely are asked to work overtime, and generous vacation time is provided for attorneys and support staff alike. In return, employees have been willing to receive slightly lower compensation than those working at other law firms. But the advantages for personal well-being are striking, as are the ripple effects upon the performance of legal services. According to one of the senior attorneys, "Rested, attuned, focused, and personally integrated employees are sharper, fresher, and less likely to make errors than those who are tired, burned-out, overworked, and whose personal lives are falling apart due to neglect . . . . [The] quality of legal services rendered is positively enhanced when the quantity is carefully controlled."[44]

If Christians' ministry of change can lead more organizations to understand and structure work in such a manner, an enormous contribution will be made to the quality of American life.

Chapter Four

Sustaining and Expanding Workplace Ministry

Sustaining and Expanding Workplace Ministry

"We experience gathering and sending like the breathing in and breathing out of the Spirit. Christian life in the everyday world is just as important as the gathering of the congregation for worship . . . . The gathering for worship serves the sending into the world, and it is this sending which leads into the full life of the Spirit."
Jürgen Moltmann, 1997[45]

Our discussion in previous chapters about why and how Christians should take faith to work leads to two final questions:

- How do we keep at it for the long run?
- What will help others make the Sunday-Monday connection?

The record of the last half century underscores the pertinence of these questions. As we saw earlier, a surge of commitment to laypeople's discipleship in the world occurred during the several decades following World War II. Challenging words were heard so frequently and promising new institutional patterns began to appear so often that, by the late 1960s, one might have thought the churches were on the eve of a new Reformation.

But, then, the deeply entrenched ways of the past reasserted themselves. A rising tide of secularism brought threats to many churches. Loss of members and of economic stability made them defensive, and their attention turned inward, to issues of institutional survival. Today, most clergy and congregations do not give a high priority to workplace ministry, and few laypeople give sustained, careful thought to how their faith relates to their work.

More importantly, however, the bold vision of the postwar years is now being recovered among a determined minority, and signs are appearing that the churches may be on the threshold of a wider and deeper commitment to the Sunday-Monday connection. It is imperative that this commitment be nourished.

My own assessment of what needs to be done to support and expand workplace ministry has led to both an encouraging answer and a discouraging one. The heartening fact is that no powerful group within the church is actively mounting deliberate opposition to this effort. Indeed, many leaders affirm its importance and some appear willing to offer support. And among the rank and file of Christian laypeople, when the challenge to take faith to work is presented, a significant minority often steps forward.

 ## An Uphill Journey

The disheartening fact is that the massive accumulated weight of many centuries, when lay ministry in the world was not a central or even normal part of the church's life, stands in the way of far-reaching change. During those years, other patterns of theological understanding, ecclesiastical practice, and personal conduct became the established norms. Today they constitute a potent barrier to lasting change.

In recent decades, thoughtful observers have studied these obstacles and offered helpful analyses of their magnitude, as well as hints of what can be done to address them effectively.

South African scholar David Bosch locates the roots of the problem deep in the church's past, in a theological perception that has held a powerful grip on Christians. From an early time in its post-apostolic history, Bosch says, the church was conceived as "a community mainly concerned with mediating eternal salvation to individuals." In this view, the "ordained ministry is the primary vehicle for that work, so the shape of the church is built around it." In the sixteenth century, the Protestant reformers initially sought a more inclusive understanding of the church's ministry, one embracing laity and clergy alike. Eventually, however, most Protestants settled for a pattern only slightly different from the traditional Catholic one: "The focus for the 'cure of souls' was not, as in Catholicism, the sacraments but the proclamation of the word of God . . . . [In] both traditions the clergyman-priest, enshrined in a privileged and central position, remained the linchpin of the church." Bosch adds that with the increased specialization of theological training begun in the nineteenth century, "the elitist character of the 'clerical paradigm' was further reinforced."[46]

Editor Celia Hahn believes an important sign of this paradigm's continuing dominance is the way laypeople's ministry tends to be regarded, like the clergy's, as occurring within the church rather than within the world. "Laity are not viewed as ministers with a distinct role . . . but as pale and inferior copies of the clergy," offering their services as "a support system for clergy ministry" within the church. A further factor accounting for this misperception, says Hahn, is that the church has slighted its mission in the world. "Since the world is out of sight, the action is confined to the church. The clergy help the laity, and the laity help out at the church. The actors in this drama are not knights doing battle in the world, but patients, nursed by the clergy and allowed to help around the ward."[47]

Loren Mead aptly describes the anomalous situation in which many clergy find themselves today. On the one hand they have begun to recognize that the laity constitutes the vanguard of the church's mission in the world, but on the other hand they are uncomfortable with the shift and "jealously guard their prerogatives." Mead continues:

> The rhetoric from the pulpit urges engagement with the world and defines one's "real" ministry as job, community life, family, etc., all of which take place *outside* the church. Yet the bulletin, the parish organization, the pastor, and staff urge and reward engagement with *parish* activities. Ministry outside the church is rarely recognized and never rewarded. Ministry inside is recognized and rewarded.[48]

Princeton University sociologist Robert Wuthnow has studied how the clergy's distance from laypeople's life in the world is played out in the church. His extensive nationwide survey in the early 1990s showed that most laypeople report receiving little help from their pastors regarding issues rising in their everyday work lives. Only one in eight (13%) would talk to their pastor about ethical problems at work; far fewer (4%) would talk to their pastor about the stress they encounter at work. Wuthnow concludes: "The clergy must do a better job of relating theology to everyday life, and they must realize that everyday life consists mostly of the work [laypeople] do in their ordinary jobs, not the work they do for an hour or two a week in the church basement."[49]

But before clergy succeed in "relating theology to everyday life," they will need more assistance from the scholars who teach them in their formative seminary years and write the books they later read. In a groundbreaking study on the issue of work written in 1991, Yale theologian Miroslav Volf acknowledges that few ethicists and theologians have tackled this field. "Amazingly little theological reflection," he reports, "has taken place in the past about an activity that takes up so much of our time." Volf then adds a telling comparison: "The number of pages theologians have devoted to the question of transubstantiation—which does or does not take place on Sunday—for instance, would, I suspect, far exceed the number of pages devoted to work that fills our lives Monday through Saturday."[50]

Presbyterian Church executive Edward A. White suggests a further dimension of the difficulty involved in bringing the changes necessary to give lay ministry in the world its due. Such a shift, White maintains, moves against the "perceived self-interest" of four parties that would be most affected—clergy, laity, theological seminaries, and secular institutions. Clergy, says White, understand their major role to consist in building up the institutional life of the church, a task for which they actively seek laypeople's support and for which they are principally evaluated and rewarded. Laypeople, in turn, find accepting their pastors' entreaties for support of the church a less demanding role than addressing the often difficult challenges involved in workplace ministry. Seminaries, for their part, concentrate more on studying the intellectual challenges that excite faculty than on nurturing in young pastors the personal and spiritual growth they will need to be faithful and courageous leaders of congregations. And the institutions of our society prefer that Christian laypeople be guided at work by the traditional values of the workplace rather than by the potentially disruptive values of the gospel.[51]

To climb beyond such barriers is a daunting task, one requiring sustained, imaginative movement on numerous fronts. Today that effort is mounting among a persistent minority of laity and clergy.

Signs of Hope

As we look quickly at this emerging effort, we should observe first that it is multifaceted and found alike in mainline and Evangelical Protestant communities, as well as in Catholic circles. One conspicuous part of it is the activity of numerous not-for-profit organizations spread around the country. Some of these "parachurch" bodies work chiefly in a single community, others sponsor programs in multiple locations. Some focus chiefly on a single vocational grouping, some embrace a wide range of vocations, and some include the whole scope of "daily life." They also vary in their choice of the word suggesting the religious component of their activity: "faith," "spirituality," and "ministry" are perhaps the three most widely used. Prominent among these organizations are the Pittsburgh Experiment, the National Center for the Laity (Chicago), the Forum for Faith in the Workplace (Columbus, Ohio), the Fellowship of Companies for Christ (Oklahoma City), the Woodstock Business Conference (Washington, D. C.), and the InterVarsity Christian Fellowship's Ministry in Daily Life (Madison, Wisconsin). As yet, relatively little consultation or coordinated planning occurs among these organizations, though personal ties have been developed among some of them, principally through their leaders' participation since the early 1990s in the Coalition for Ministry in Daily Life.

The programs of these groups have been fed in part by the recent work of Christian scholars, especially those who have begun to write about the theology, spirituality, and ethics of work. The important new body of literature they are creating includes such volumes as Lee Hardy, *The Fabric of This World: Inquiries into Calling, Career Choice and the Design of Human Work* (1990); Miroslav Volf, *Work in the Spirit: Toward a Theology of*

Work (1991); Laura L. Nash, *Believers in Business* (1994); James
M. Childs, Jr., *Ethics in Business: Faith at Work* (1995); R. Paul
Stevens, *The Other Six Days: Vocation, Work, and Ministry in
Biblical Perspective* (1999); Robert Banks and Kimberly Powell,
eds., *Faith in Leadership: How Leaders Live Out Their Faith In Their
Work and Why It Matters* (2000); and Gregory F. A. Pierce,
spirituality@work: 10 ways to balance your life on-the-job (2001).[52]

This impressive theological output has been paralleled by a
significant succession of volumes by corporate executives
explaining their diverse perspectives on the faith-work
connection. Notable examples include Robert K. Greenleaf,
*Servant Leadership: A Journey into the Nature of Legitimate Power
and Greatness* (1977); Max De Pree, *Leadership Is an Art* (1989);
Tom Chappell, *The Soul of a Business: Managing for Profit and the
Common Good* (1993); James A. Autry, *Life & Work: A Manager's
Search for Meaning* (1994); and C. William Pollard, *The Soul of
the Firm* (1996).

Another sign of hope is the rising interest of congregations
in the Sunday-Monday connection. As yet, the numbers are
small and few contacts exist among those leading the way.
Nor has a systematic study been done of their activity. In these
places, however, one finds exemplary efforts to awaken and
support Christians' following of Christ in the world of work.
Prominent examples include an Episcopal parish in San Francisco
noted by Robert Bellah in *Habits of the Heart* (1985);
a Lutheran congregation in Emmaus, Pennsylvania, described in
detail by William Diehl in *Ministry in Daily Life: A Practical
Guide for Congregations* (1996); and a Presbyterian congregation
near Santa Barbara, California, pastored by Steve Jacobsen and
reflected in his book, *Hearts to God, Hands to Work: Connecting
Spirituality and Work* (1997).

An especially promising development is the attention of
Luther Seminary in St. Paul, Minnesota, to ways that
congregations can support members' ongoing ministry in daily
life. Established in 1999, the school's Centered Life Initiative

works with a growing number of congregations to help them develop and use carefully tailored resources in worship, education, and outreach. The intention, says Executive Director Jack Fortin, is to build a new paradigm for congregations. Merely gathering and caring for members is not enough, he contends; each congregation also must challenge members to discern God's calling to them in the world, then support them as they seek to implement their callings in everyday life.

Luther Seminary's active interest in the Sunday-Monday connection is unusual among American theological schools, but Luther is not the only seminary that includes this set of issues within its educational mission. Today, similar efforts are under way at Fuller Theological Seminary (in California), Gordon Conwell Theological Seminary (in Massachusetts), and Yale Divinity School (in Connecticut). The beginnings at these four schools are modest, but as their initiatives grow and prompt other seminaries to comparable ventures, the potential harvest is immense.

Clearly, these diverse efforts are both responding to and feeding a growing interest among lay and ordained Christians across the nation. Scholarly analysis of this grassroots interest has been provided by two sociological studies performed between 1989 and 1992. One of them, conducted by the Center for Ethics and Corporate Policy, analyzed a cross-section of Christian opinion and practice present among 158 congregations in the metropolitan Chicago area. It found that although most respondents connect faith to work less than to the other spheres of their lives, they nevertheless do recognize the importance of making such a linkage. "There is strong and widespread desire," the study's authors concluded, "for congregational support and guidance in integrating faith and work."[53]

The other project, noted earlier, was carried out by Robert Wuthnow and the Princeton University Center for the Study of Religion. It gathered data from across the United States regarding Christians' practices and attitudes on several key economic matters. Wuthnow and his colleagues discovered that although most clergy are overwhelmed by the complexity of their parishioners' daily involvement in work-related issues, they nevertheless do want to help laity relate faith to this part of their lives. But the clergy's doing so is handicapped by the fact that many of them have little knowledge of parishioners' work lives. Moreover, in their uncertainty they have settled for repeating the therapeutic counsel of some secular sources regarding work issues (such as "do what will make you happy") rather than offering the distinctive wisdom of the Christian tradition. Wuthnow adds that the clergy's failure to provide greater assistance to laypeople in this realm is a major reason laypeople do not participate in congregations more actively and give to them more generously. He believes that if clergy were to become better versed in helping laypeople connect their faith and their work lives, this could be a key step toward overcoming the "spiritual malaise" and "fiscal woe" that together constitute what he views as "the crisis in the churches."[54]

How can these signs of hope be sustained and multiplied? How can they engage a growing circle of Christians in the task of connecting faith and work? My own experience shows that the exact ways individuals and groups can best carry out this effort will vary considerably, depending on their circumstances and their particular gifts. The opportunities for some are greater than for others; so, too, the difficulties. But no Christian is without a role.

As I view the possibilities for moving forward, I see three realms as especially important for a strategic focusing of effort—among individuals, among congregations, and among theological schools.

A Matter of Personal Commitment

Every individual who discovers God's call to workplace ministry must make a personal assessment of the new paths now to be explored and the old ones to be abandoned. The particularities of these decisions will be unique for each person, because each of us has a distinctive set of opportunities and limitations. Each must determine before God where this journey will lead. Each must also recognize our accountability to God for how faithfully we persist in our commitment. And, because each person who is joined to Christ is also joined to other Christians, we should seek each other's support, both in embarking on the journey and in continuing on it.

Some who read these pages will be well along in the process, others will be in the early stages. For the latter group, particularly, I offer several suggestions about what can be done to help sustain the commitment to workplace ministry and to encourage others to make and keep the same commitment.

Most critical is the safeguarding and nurturing of the vision of the Sunday-Monday connection given to us. The many demands upon our time and energy will tempt us to back away from this vision, perhaps assigning it a low priority among our commitments. It is very easy to convince ourselves to wait until we have more time or until the climate at work or in the congregation is more favorable. Such temptations must be resisted stoutly, for the vision is from God and we are its stewards.

Two practical suggestions perhaps will be useful here, one concerning a group process, the other an individual process. Both should be considered, for they complement each other. The group process requires each of us to find at least one other person who will help us stay in touch with the spiritual depths from which our personal commitment to workplace ministry springs, as well as explore the particular work-related issues that concern us most. Such a support process perhaps can be developed best among a small circle of Christians who discover that they share this commitment, and then begin meeting regularly, with workplace issues being the center holding them together. Or it may be preferable that an already existing support group include this issue among the ones that its members address.

For the first type—a continuing association of individuals focused on workplace ministry—various models have proved fruitful.

1. William Diehl has long been part of a group from his Lutheran congregation in Pennsylvania called "The Monday Connection." Its members, coming from different workplaces, have a hour-long breakfast meeting the first Monday of the month. One person each time comes ready to share a tough problem he or she is encountering (or previously has encountered) in the workplace. The others then explore with that person how the gospel relates to the problem. The congregation's pastor is a regular participant.[55]

2. Some people have found value in meeting regularly with fellow Christians who work within the same organization, usually gathering at lunchtime for Bible study and prayer.

3. Organizations such as the Pittsburgh Experiment and the Forum for Faith in the Workplace have taken the lead in bringing Christians together at mealtime from different nearby workplaces for weekly sharing of personal stories, discussion of the gospel's bearing on workplace quandaries, and prayer.

4. Some Evangelical CEOs have developed a support network maintained chiefly through modern telecommunications, with conference calls being scheduled monthly for discussion of tough business issues and prayer.[56]

5. Catholic businessman William Farley helped form a support circle of Hartford business leaders who meet monthly to discuss issues facing the local business community. "We talk about how to make our work more Christian. When I'm faced with a decision I can think: What would Jack do? What would Myron do? What might the Lord do?"[57]

Many of these groups draw participants chiefly from the business world. But this is not the only pattern. Theologian Gabriel Fackre tells about a discussion group comprised mostly of scientists. All were members of the same congregation outside Boston. They gathered regularly over a several-year period to explore the gospel's meaning for their work on the frontiers of science. Fackre met with them and provides a picture of the issues they addressed:

Each evening a different member takes the "hot seat" to talk about his or her work. Frank reported on the breakthroughs in gene splicing in his experiments at MIT. Al tested out with the group a code of ethics he developed for cancer research. Jill described a new strain of corn being studied in her laboratory and the impact it could have on hunger in Third World countries. George told of his misgivings about his company's new MX missile contract. Bill brought charts and graphs to get feedback on his effort to widen employee decision-making power in the small firm he had founded. Sandra explained the dilemmas of many science teachers these days as they struggle with the creationist-evolutionist controversy. Carl shared his attempt to alert fellow pediatricians to the medical effects of a nuclear attack and the need for a freeze on this weaponry.[58]

The other, complementary process of support and nurture concerns us more as individuals. Each of us must find ways to commune regularly with God and to let that relationship inform our reflections on our particular ways of making the Sunday-Monday connection. The pace of life today makes such discipline hard to establish and perhaps harder to maintain, but finding a pattern suitable to each person's circumstances and temperament is critical.

A range of possibilities needs to be considered. Where a pattern of personal discipline already exists, it should be relatively easy to assimilate the issues of workplace discipleship into it. Where no pattern currently exists, it probably would be helpful to experiment with different options before settling on the one that works best.

One option to consider comes from business executive William Diehl's experience. Here is how he describes his own pattern of morning prayer and reflection:

Every morning I allocate about twenty minutes for meditation. That means the alarm clock must be set accordingly, depending upon what my schedule is for that day . . . . I usually go downstairs to a favorite chair and first read from whatever book I am working my way through . . . . Putting the book down, I pause to reflect on how the words I have just read relate to the events of my day. Sometimes there are startling connections; sometimes there is nothing . . . .

Then I turn to prayer. I begin by giving thanks, and that is easy for all of us, for there is so much for which we can be thankful. Then comes a period of personal intercessory prayer for Judy, my wife, and all our children and grandchildren . . . .

Finally I turn to my agenda for the day. I go down the list of things scheduled for the day . . . . For each of these scheduled events, I pray that I may be open to the possibilities of carrying out ministry with and to those with whom I will come in contact. My closing petition is that my own ego and selfish desires will be pushed aside to make way for the will of God and the presence of Jesus.[59]

Some Christians may prefer a pattern of spiritual discipline less dependent on the availability of periods of undisturbed quiet. Catholic publisher Gregory Pierce has led the way in developing a pattern of disciplined reflection he believes is better suited to the busy pace of the layperson's life today than are the traditional contemplative disciplines developed in earlier times by clergy and monks. This "spirituality of work" helps one find God in the workplace and strive there, Pierce says, to make the world a better place, "a little closer to the way God would have things."

For Pierce this pattern of spirituality is comprised of ten disciplines that he believes can be practiced by most laypeople in their workplaces.

> Surrounding yourself with "sacred" objects
> Living with imperfection
> Assuring quality
> Giving thanks and congratulations
> Building support and community
> Dealing with others as you would have them deal with you
> Deciding what is "enough"—and sticking to it

Balancing work, personal, family, church, and
   community responsibilities
Working to make "the system" work
Engaging in ongoing personal and professional
   development[60]

A striking feature of Pierce's proposal is its formulation by him through an on-line process of dialogue with several hundred people sharing his wish to find and serve God in the midst of daily work.

 ## Involving the Congregation

Keeping the flame burning in one's own mind and spirit is essential, but it is not enough. Taking faith to work is a critical part of the whole church's mission and must become a more central part of every congregation's life. Hence, we must seek ways to awaken this commitment among fellow Christians in every congregation, in every place where the church of Jesus Christ is present—including those Christians whose traditions speak of "the parish" rather than "the congregation." This clearly is a demanding task, but thanks to the efforts of pioneers who have gone before us, it is increasingly evident how it should be approached.

In view of the leadership role played by pastors within most congregations, an essential prerequisite for sustained congregational engagement is support by the pastor. No blueprint exists to tell unfailingly how this support can be won or how it can be best expressed. The experience of Steve Jacobsen, a Presbyterian pastor in California, is perhaps typical of many clergy who embark in a new direction. He tells what happened in his own mind when the light came that showed him the inadequacy of his old ways.

> I began to be aware that my habits of mind led me to perpetuate a sense that the world of God and the world of work are unrelated.
> I became aware of how rarely my sermons referred to the world of work and how little my teaching ministry touched on these concerns.
> I began to realize how often the issues people struggle with involve in some way jobs, money, and vocation.
> As I reflected on my own children and the youth at my church, I realized we were doing nothing to equip them for the soul-work necessary for integrating faith and work.[61]

Jacobsen's statement bears a moment's reflection. At the time of his turnaround he recognized that he had been neglecting an important realm of Christian truth and discipleship, not because a sinister or irresistible force opposed it, but because the past had shaped his thought patterns ("my habits of mind") in such a way that he was blinded to this realm. He also realized that paying attention to workplace issues would, in fact, bring him into closer contact with a part of life critical to younger and older people alike in his congregation. And he realized, finally, that what he must do to implement his changed awareness required less a new set of activities than the penetration of what he was already doing (his sermons and teaching ministry) with a fresh perspective.

Steve Jacobsen suggests that an instructive way of viewing the congregation is to think of it as the base camp for a hiking expedition. Everything that goes on is aimed at preparing hikers for their climb up the mountain. Jacobsen explains:

The church is a base camp in which a community of people gathers to reflect on life, be reminded of their identity, and make plans for exploration. From there, each person goes out during the week to take on that part of the mountain that is theirs to explore. The base camp exists to serve the climbing team. In itself, it is neither the goal of the expedition nor the mountain itself. The value of this image is that it affirms the importance of the community and institution but it does not mistake the institution for the central reality. The hikers don't exist for the good of the base camp. The base camp exists for the good of the hikers.[62]

Jacobsen, Diehl and other pioneers have developed numerous practical ways that this "base camp" can prepare Christians for their ministries in the workplace.

The most critical factor is the pastor's determination to make his or her own ministry relevant to people's everyday work lives, so they know themselves affirmed, equipped, and supported as they embark on their respective ministries in the workplace. An indispensable step in this direction is for the pastor to become better informed about the work issues that dominate the waking hours of most laity. This can be done through such practices as regular reading of publications that focus on work and economic issues (the *Wall Street Journal* or the business section of the local newspaper are good beginning points); visiting parishioners in their places of work (perhaps best scheduled for lunchtime); pursuing a continuing education project that addresses this set of issues; and encouraging members of the congregation to talk about their work issues in church settings, partly to teach their pastor and partly to remind themselves that work issues are also faith issues.

It is important, too, for pastors to recognize that the parish itself is a workplace, in some respects similar to the workplaces in which most parishioners spend their days. As administrators, caregivers, and teachers, the men and women who are pastors may well have more in common with working lay members than they have realized.

Sunday morning worship can be a time rich in affirmation of lay ministry. The range of possibilities includes such steps as the pastor's regular use of workplace-based illustrations in sermons and inclusion of workplace issues in pastoral prayers; invitations to laypeople to lead the congregation with their own work-related prayers; and periodic commissioning of groups of laity who share the same vocational focus (for example, all those working in educational settings—including support staff such as secretaries, cafeteria workers, and custodians) for their ministries on behalf of Christ at their places of work.

More fundamentally, the pastor and other congregational leaders must help all who worship to experience this holy time of Word and Sacrament as the occasion for renewing themselves for the service of God and neighbor throughout the week. We must learn and relearn that the God we meet Sunday morning is the God who desires to meet us every day at work. "Where is God?" asks an ancient Jewish text. "Where you let God in," is the answer.[63]

A congregation's education program also provides opportunities to address the theme of workplace ministry. Adult classes can regularly undertake study of this topic, and some have made it the focus of fruitful day-long and overnight retreats. Especially critical is the need to develop discussion of this issue among young people as they start to think about getting a job and preparing themselves for their work lives. Confirmation training can be an excellent time for them to begin asking how work relates to God's purpose for their lives and what gifts they have received from God for their careers.

Explorers of the workplace ministry frontier have identified a wide range of additional ways congregations can affirm and support this aspect of Christian discipleship. Some, for example, include an individual's occupation and place of work in the congregational membership roster. Some offer regular gifts- and vocation-discernment workshops for members. Some routinely include work-life stories (by members as well as outsiders) in congregational newsletters. Some annually make the Sunday after Labor Day a time for focusing on members' workplace ministry. The point to be remembered is that because of chronic neglect of this part of Christians' lives, many members do not yet see it as a part of their discipleship, and even for those who do, it often is not clear how they should go about the daily task of taking faith to work. Constant reminders and support are necessary.

 Engaging Theological Schools

A key resource to be developed for the churches' affirmation and undergirding of workplace ministry is the realm of theological education.

The approximately 200 accredited theological seminaries and divinity schools in North America are now chiefly invested in the important work of preparing men and women for careers as ordained ministers. With current priorities and chronic financial burdens demanding the full energy of their leaders, it is a rare theological educator who considers expansion of a school's mission in the direction of lay ministry in the world. William Diehl tells of a friend who inquired about the possibility of such expansion. When Pastor Al Roberts asked a seminary dean about his school's readiness to address this issue, the dean replied that he would invite an outsider to give a lecture and possibly develop a course. Lamenting the tepidness of this response, Roberts went on to ask, "When will the seminary begin to examine how it prepares pastors so that they have some clue as to their role in helping plumbers minister to other plumbers, carpenters minister to other carpenters, and nurses minister to other nurses, and to developing a cadre . . . that is a launching pad for the real ministry of the church?" To this question the dean responded, "Well, we're not quite that far along yet."[64]

In the 1970s one seminary in the United States was far enough along that it seriously addressed this issue. Andover Newton Theological School, affiliated with the United Church of Christ and located near Boston, initially undertook a five-year process of exploration ("the Laity Project"), under the direction of Richard Broholm. Then, in 1980, it inaugurated a groundbreaking Center for the Ministry of the Laity. Engaging seminary faculty with pastors and laity from surrounding churches, the Center sponsored a variety of occasions for participants to think freshly about lay ministry in the work world and to experiment with new patterns of action. Regrettably, after the sudden death in 1990 of George Peck, who was both the seminary president and chief advocate of the Center (and whose passing occurred about the same time as the deaths of two other key supporters), this initiative lost financial backing and soon ended.

But in its years of innovation and experimentation, the Andover Newton venture gleaned intriguing learnings. During that time of ferment, George Peck wrote about his discoveries:

> [Laypeople's] minds teemed with striking theological and spiritual insight, with a vital, thoughtful appreciation for the issues involved in what they were doing as believers, all made fresher and more forceful because they came with a perspective that was different from my "professional" outlook. I realized very quickly that, as an ordained person, I had never really learned to *hear* the laity. I had become much too accustomed simply to *talking* to them . . . .

I was quickly challenged and convicted by their obvious sense that by and large the church did not take them seriously in their quest for ministry and did not support or undergird them . . . . [They] had to look beyond the church if they were to find the stimulus and reinforcement they needed to carry out their ministry in the midst of the workaday world . . . .

I found it hard to avoid the unpleasant impression that, despite our good intentions, we who are ordained are often the very ones in the church who do not take the laity seriously . . . . [We] project the impression that, if the laity have a ministry, it is to be carried on within the household of faith, not in the world . . . .

I found myself wondering what would happen if our churchly agenda were to be determined by the fact that one of our fundamental tasks is to prepare, commission, support and hold accountable all the members in their ministry between Monday and Saturday . . . . What if, for its own upbuilding toward its mission, the church found ways to draw upon the rich store of understanding, insight and expertise that is already there, but underutilized, in all its members?[65]

Peck's observations constitute seed that may yet bear fruit in theological schools ready to make exploration of the Sunday-Monday connection an important part of their educational mission. As yet, too little experimentation has occurred to know clearly how they can best reshape their programs of intellectual and spiritual formation to take on this task. My own hunches, based on many years as a seminary professor, lead me to believe that certain innovative steps could prove extremely productive. They bear on both the processes and content of theological education.

For example, those who oversee the processes of theological education should find ways:

- For non-ordination track laypeople to become regular participants in the schools' courses, both for what they can impart and for what they can learn (without expecting lay participants to do what a retired GE senior executive told me had been expected of him in an ethics course—"to park my experience at the door")
- For ordination-track students to have field education and internship opportunities in secular work environments (beyond the hospital settings in which some already work)
- For clergy and laypeople to have continuing education opportunities addressing workplace issues

Those who provide the content of theological education should find ways:

- For theology, Scripture, and ethics courses to address questions relating to God's involvement with the world of work
- For church history courses to analyze the reasons for and consequences of the spiritualizing of the gospel and the clericalizing of the church's life
- For practice of ministry courses to deal with the clergy's equipping role in the congregation and with the laity's ministry in the workaday world

Because theological schools are important in shaping the future of Christianity, their leaders are lobbied often by diverse constituents to take on issues and tasks they think will help the churches better serve the Christian cause. Not all of these voices can be heeded. Choices must be made. For those schools able to look beyond the pressures of the moment to what the shape of the churches' engagement with the world must be in coming years, the time is ripe for establishing a new priority: to teach future clergy that a key part of their ministry must be to help laypeople discover their own ministries in the workplaces of the world.

 ## Moving Toward the Future

As we look to what can be done to shape the future, it needs to be remembered that the ways Christians can begin to implement the Sunday-Monday connection are numerous and varied. Some of those ways are immediately within reach, only a soul-beat away. They are as accessible as changing how I relate to a workplace colleague tomorrow or recasting what I say in church next Sunday.

The critical factor is one's determination to persist in the simple changes, then to take, bit by bit, the more far-reaching steps that, joined to the initiatives of others, will contribute to a groundswell capable of reshaping attitudes, teachings, and practices. With the Spirit's blessing, such incremental progress can eventually bring a time when taking faith to work is a normal part of Christian life.

The patience and determination necessary for that long journey can be helpfully nourished by a sense of history. Loren Mead reminds us that the term "ministry of the laity" occurred for the first time in modern usage in the 1930s. Those years, he continues, "were only yesterday in the life of an institution that measures change in generations and centuries. It is a brand new idea still—an idea yet to have its full impact on us."[66]

Christian history abounds in instances of gradual movement toward major achievements. About two hundred years ago, for example, small groups of Christians made discoveries that were effectively shared with others and eventually had far-reaching impacts. One group saw that the gospel is meant to be communicated to the whole human family, not just to the people of western Christendom. Another group saw that the gospel condemns the practice of slavery. And a third group saw that Christ calls women to full citizenship rights in church and society alike.

Perhaps when future generations of Christians look back upon the early years of the twentieth-first century, they will see it as another pivotal time in Christian history, when a neglected dimension of the gospel was effectively championed, a growing number of Christian laypeople took faith to work, and things were never again the same.

Endnotes

1. Bosch, *Transforming Mission: Paradigm Shifts in Theology of Mission* (Orbis Books, 1991), p. 467.

2. Hendrik Kraemer, *A Theology of the Laity* (Westminster Press, 1958), pp. 111, 113-114.

3. "Spiritualizing" has been helpfully analyzed in Jürgen Moltmann, *The Source of Life: The Holy Spirit and the Theology of Life* (Fortress Press, 1997); on "clericalizing" see Paul M. Minus, "Lay Movements," *Encyclopedia of Christianity*, vol. 3 (Brill/Eerdmanns, 2003).

4. *Evanston Speaks: Reports of the Second Assembly of the World Council of Churches* (WCC, 1955), pp. 59-60, 64-65.

5. Walter J. Abbott, ed., *Documents of Vatican II* (Herder and Herder/Association Press, 1966), Dogmatic Constitution on the Church, section 31, pp. 57-58; Pastoral Constitution on the Church in the Modern World, section 38, p. 236.

6. This important development is addressed in Bosch, *Transforming Mission*, esp. Part 3.

7. Loren B. Mead, *The Once and Future Church: Reinventing the Congregation for a New Mission Frontier* (The Alban Institute, Inc. 1991), p. 24.

8. The chief study making this point is Robert Wuthnow, *The Crisis in the Churches: Spiritual Malaise, Fiscal Woe* (Oxford University Press, 1997).

9. Diehl, *The Monday Connection: On Being an Authentic Christian in a Weekday World* (HarperSanFrancisco, 1991). Diehl's retrospective comment quoted above appears on p. 10.

10. Trueblood, *Your Other Vocation* (Harper and Brothers, 1952), pp. 57-58.

11. As, for example, in Ephesians 6:12 and Colossians 2:15.

12. Terkel, *Working: People Talk About What They Do All Day and How They Feel About What They Do* (Ballantine Books edition, 1985), p. xiii.

13. A recent study of this phenomenon is Laura Nash and Scotty McLennan, *Church on Sunday, Work on Monday: The Challenge of Fusing Christian Values with Business Life* (Jossey-Bass, 2001). The authors conclude that a major factor turning business leaders away from the churches is the anti-capitalist bias of many clergy.

14. Satullo, "Lay Ministry Battle Story: Grey Areas in Black Type," in Verna Dozier, ed., *The Calling of the Laity* (The Alban Institute, Inc. 1988), pp. 10-11.

15. The first De Pree quote is from Laura L. Nash, *Believers in Business* (Thomas Nelson Publishers, 1994), p. 262; the second quote is from Max De Pree, *Leading Without Power: Finding Hope in Serving Community* (Jossey-Bass Publishers, 1997), p. 172.

16. Sandra Herron, "Reflecting Christ in the Banking Industry: The Manager as Prophet, Priest and King," in Robert J. Banks, ed., *Faith Goes to Work: Reflections from the Marketplace* (The Alban Institute, Inc. 1993), pp. 83, 85.

17. Chappell, *The Soul of a Business: Managing for Profit and the Common Good* (Bantam Books, 1993), pp. x, 202.

18. Cited in Tom Sullivan and Al Gini, *Heigh-Ho, Heigh-Ho: Funny, Insightful, Encouraging and Sometimes Painful Quotes About Work* (Acta Publications, 1994), p. 56.

19. Cited in Lee Hardy, *The Fabric of This World: Inquiries into Calling, Career Choice, and the Design of Human Work* (Eerdman's Publishing Co. 1990), p. 100.

20. Cited in William L. Droel, *The Spirituality of Work: Business People* (ACTA Publications, 1991), p. 25.

21. Robert Wuthnow, *God and Mammon in America* (The Free Press, 1994), p. 49.

22. Richard N. Bolles, *What Color is Your Parachute? A Practical Manual for Job-Hunters and Career-Changers* (Ten Speed Press, 1999), p. 254.

23. De Pree, *Leadership Is an Art* (Dell Trade Paperback, 1989), p. 32; Handy, *Waiting for the Mountain to Move: Reflections on Work and Life* (Jossey-Bass Publisher, 1999), p. 38.

24. Chappell, *Soul*, p. 60.

25. Dennis, "Compassion is the Most Vital Tool of My Trade," in Gregory F. Augustine Pierce, ed., *Of Human Hands: A Reader in the Spirituality of Work* (Augsburg, 1991), pp. 49-51.

26. Finn, "Hazardous Waste and Holy Ground," in Dozier, ed., *The Calling*, p. 60.

27. Newbold, "To Walk with Each One," in Pierce, ed., *Of Human Hands*, p. 100.

28. Dunne, "My Faith Helps with the Important Work," in *Ibid.*, p. 79.

29. Cited in Linda L. Granz and J. Fletcher Lowe, eds., *Ministry in Daily Life: A Guide to Living the Baptismal Covenant* (The Episcopal Church, 1996), p. 177.

30. Pope John Paul II, in his 1981 encyclical *On Human Work* (Laborem Exercens).

31. The first statement cited is from James Patterson and Peter Kim, *The Day America Told the Truth* (Prentice Hall Press, 1991), p. 237. The other source referred to is Robert Putnam, *Bowling Alone: The Collapse and Revival of American Community* (Simon and Schuster, 2000) p. 25.

32. Volf's comment is from his book, *Work in the Spirit: Toward a Theology of Work* (Oxford University Press, 1991), p. 7. The Volf volume is an important step toward addressing the "deficiency." See also Gilbert C. Meilaender, ed., *Working: Its Meaning and Limits* (University of Notre Dame Press, 2000) and Pete Hammond, Paul Stevens, and Todd Svanoe, *The Marketplace Annotated Bibliography: A Christian Guide to Books on Work, Business and Vocation* (InterVarsity Press, 2002).

33. Autry, *Life and Work: A Manager's Search for Meaning* (Avon Books, 1994), p. 33.

34. James M. Childs, Jr., *Ethics in Business: Faith at Work* (Fortress Press, 1995), p. 134.

35. Cited in Nash, *Believers in Business*, pp. 88-90.

36. Herron, "Reflecting Christ," p. 85.

37. De Pree, *Leadership*, pp. 119-120.

38. *Ibid.*, p. 48.

39. Patti Amy, in a 1998 essay prepared to meet requirements for a course on "Faith in the Workplace" I co-taught at the Methodist Theological School in Ohio.

40. Schor, *The Overworked American: The Unexpected Decline of Leisure* (Basic Books, 1992), pp. 11-12.

41. Hardy, *Fabric of This World*, pp. xvi, 113.

42. From the pope's encyclical, *Mater et Magistra*, cited in *Ibid.*, pp. 127-8.

43. *Ibid.*, p. 174.

44. *Ibid.*, pp. 109-110.

45. Moltmann, *The Source of Life*, pp. 95-96.

46. Bosch, *Transforming Mission*, pp. 469-70.

47. Hahn, "Where in the World is the Church?" in Dozier, ed., *The Calling of the Laity*, p. 89.

48. Mead, *Once and Future Church*, pp. 34-35.

49. Wuthnow, *Crisis in the Churches*, pp. 62, 7.

50. Volf, *Work in the Spirit*, p. 69.

51. White, "The Sunday-Monday Gap," in Banks, ed., *Faith Goes to Work*, pp. 5-11.

52. Further information about these books and several others cited in the next two paragraphs is included in the Bibliography.

53. Stephen Hart and David Krueger, "Faith and Work: Challenges for Congregations," *The Christian Century*, July 15-22, 1992, p. 685.

54. Wuthnow, *Crisis in the Churches*, pp. 71-86.

55. Diehl, *Ministry in Daily Life*, pp. 43-45.

56. Nash, *Believers in Business*, pp. 50, 187.

57. Droel, *Spirituality of Work: Business People*, p. 54.

58. Fackre, "Christ's Ministry and Ours," in George Peck and John S. Hoffman, eds., *The Laity in Ministry: The Whole People of God for the Whole World* (Judson Press, 1984), p. 109.

59. Diehl, *In Search of Faithfulness: Lessons from the Christian Community* (Fortress Press, 1987), pp. 56-58.

60. Pierce, *spirituality@work*, p. v.

61. Jacobsen, *Hearts to God*, p. x.

62. *Ibid.*, p. 24.

63. Jeffrey K. Salkin, *Being God's Partner: How to Find the Hidden Link Between Spirituality and Your Work* (Jewish Lights Publishing, 1994), p. 58.

64. Diehl, *Ministry in Daily Life*, p. 66.

65. Peck, "Reconceiving the Ministry of the Laity: A Personal Testimony," in Peck and Hoffman, eds., *Laity in Ministry*, pp. 15-17.

66. Mead, *Once and Future Church*, p. 24.

Study Aids:
An Overview

Study Aids: An Overview

Taking Faith to Work has been prepared for use in a variety of settings—by individuals reading on their own, as well as by groups engaged in a pattern of disciplined study and discussion. The study guides in the following pages have been developed chiefly with groups of 10-12 participants in mind, but with some modification they also can be used in smaller or larger group settings. Individual readers will find the guides a helpful tool for personal study as they pause to reflect on questions, quotes, or prayers that strike home.

These Study Aids have been divided into five parts, with the first part intended to be used in conjunction with the book's Introduction, and with each of the following parts intended to be used in conjunction with each of the four succeeding chapters.

Groups that already exist (such as church school classes and Bible study groups) should be able to make constructive use of this book as part of their regular meetings. But it should be possible, also, to use it in groups that are formed specifically for consideration of the issues raised here. Normally, it will probably be most effective to spend five (or more) successive sessions on the five parts; but experience has shown that some may find it preferable to tackle *Taking Faith to Work* at a retreat lasting a full day or longer. Others may be constrained by scheduling pressures to fit it into a shorter time frame.

Whatever the pattern chosen, the most critical requirement for fruitful study is the commitment of group members to active participation. This means engaging in careful reading between sessions, then in thoughtful speaking and listening at meetings. It also means adhering to the commitments agreed upon at the first meeting regarding such matters as respect, confidentiality, and so forth.

Each part of the Study Aids begins with a brief statement of *Objectives* for the session ahead. Then comes a recommended *Fellowship Activity* connected to faith-work themes. This start-up exercise will help build relationships and encourage sharing; it sets the stage for the substantive discussion that follows.

Questions for Discussion, Grist, and *Case Studies* are intended to consume the bulk of the group's meeting time. They provide an opportunity to review, reflect upon, and digest key parts of each chapter. Groups should use the parts that are most pertinent, not necessarily all of them. If other important items for discussion emerge within the group, take time to pursue them.

For the Next Time provides a brief opportunity toward the end of the meeting to highlight themes that will be covered in the next session, as well as to make clear the "homework" expectations.

Each meeting ends with a *Closing* devotional moment that reinforces learning that has occurred and underscores the sacred meaning of our work.

The amount of time that groups have available for each session will vary greatly. It is recommended that, where five sessions are scheduled, about ninety minutes (if possible) be devoted to each of the first four sessions, and approximately two hours to the final session. The extra time at the end will allow response to whatever "wrap-up" and "where-do-we-go-from-here" considerations that are appropriate.

Study Aids for Use With Introduction

Objectives

- To get acquainted with each other and share thoughts about work
- To explore why connecting faith and work can be difficult, and why doing it is important
- To agree on logistical details about the group's future sessions (time, location, assignments between meetings, and so forth)

Fellowship activity

Host/facilitator welcomes participants and invites each person to share information about him- or herself, including but not limited to:

- Name
- Occupation or primary work role (last occupation if not working now)
- Other important roles (for example, parent, church council, baseball coach)
- Why I'm participating
- My first paying job and its impact on me

Ground rules

For a group to function effectively, members must understand one another's expectations and agree on how the group is to function. It will be helpful to talk briefly about the commitments that will guide participants' interaction with each other. Here are some possibilities to consider:

- **Participation** – Everyone participates and no one dominates; members agree to attend all sessions if possible and to notify the facilitator or meeting host if it will be necessary to miss a session.

- **Respect** – Everyone has experience and ideas that deserve to be shared.
- **Confidentiality** – Anything said of a personal or sensitive nature stays within the group.
- **Preparation** – Optimal discussion and learning will occur only if everyone completes the brief reading assignment (including the Study Aids) prior to each meeting.

Questions for discussion

1. In his book, *The Monday Connection* (p. 1), William Diehl says that "Most Christians are unable to bring into the experiences of everyday life the basic elements of the faith they profess on a Sunday morning. When asked how the experiences of 11:00 a.m. on Monday connect with what they experienced at 11:00 a.m. on Sunday in church, most Christians are at a total loss for words." Do you agree with Diehl? If so, what do you think has brought about this situation? What are the chief ways you currently relate your faith to your work?

2. What are some ways you have known God's presence in your life outside the workplace—in a particularly memorable event, in the beauty of nature, in a remarkable experience with another person, and so forth? When similar things happen in your workplace, are you as likely to see God's presence in them? Should you? Why, or why not?

3. Is there an issue or relationship at work that is particularly troubling to you which you hope this study process will help you deal with? Can you share it with the group?

4. In what ways does your congregation/pastor help people deal with problems at work? How can more help be provided?

5. Are there other issues raised in this first reading that you would like the group to discuss?

Grist for further reflection and discussion

"*Myth:* Work is a part of the curse . . . . *Fact:* Work is a gift from God. The Bible never calls work a curse, but rather a gift from God (Ecclesiastes 3:13; 5:18-19) . . . . God gave Adam and Eve work to do long before they ever sinned (Genesis 2:15) and He commands and commends work long after their fall (Genesis 9:1-7; Colossians 3:23; 1 Thessalonians 4:11)."

From *Word in Life Bible* (Thomas Nelson Publishers, 1998), p. 1792.

"The road to holiness for most of us lies in our secular vocation . . . . Our faith . . . is a pervasive reality to be practiced every day in homes, offices, factories, schools, and businesses across our land. We cannot separate what we believe from how we act in the marketplace."

From National Conference of Catholic Bishops, *Economic Justice for All: Pastoral Letter on Catholic Social Teaching and the U.S. Economy* (NCCB, 1986), pp. xiv-xv.

"The Bible has, in fact, more to say about daily chores than most of its readers realize . . . . Our first glimpse of man is as a farmer, cultivating and conserving the ground (Genesis 2:15). Every glimpse of God shows Him as a mighty worker who brings new things into existence and untiringly oversees all the enterprises in His vast domain. In accomplishing His greatest work, God sends a carpenter to construct a city into which men will bring the fruits of all their labors. There are vivid pictures, as well, of God's adversary, who plants weeds in the same field and erects towers in the same city. But at the end the works of

God's servants will 'follow them,' and supreme among them all is the perfected work of God's Son. A book by workers, about workers, for workers—that is the Bible!"

Paul S. Minear, in John Oliver Nelson, ed., *Work and Vocation: A Christian Discussion* (Harper, 1954), p. 33.

For the next time

- Set meeting date and location, leadership responsibilities, and so forth for the next session.
- The next session will look more closely at the disconnect between faith and work, explore its origins and consequences, and begin to connect Sunday to Monday. During the coming week look for ways you might connect faith to your work and/or perceived barriers to doing so.
- Participants should read Chapter One and the appropriate Study Aids prior to the next session.

Closing

The group may well want to end the session with prayer, thereby helping the heart embrace what the head has said and heard. Prayers perhaps will emerge from within the group. Here is one that might also be used (to be prayed in unison).

> *Thank you, God, for those who, like you,*
> *repair our homes and our hearts;*
> *for electricians who fix our wiring and restore*
> *power lines;*
> *for surgeons who repair blocked arteries and*
> *remove tumors;*
> *for plumbers who unclog drains and fix leaking pipes;*
> *for therapists who dispel the demons of our mind.*
>
> *Thank you, God for those who, like your Son,*
> *teach and guide us;*

for teachers who give our children knowledge;
for saints who have taught us the true meaning
   of faith;
for professors who have challenged and pushed us
   to think;
for dads and moms who teach us to be
   uncommonly wise.

Thank you, God, for those who, like your Word,
   enrich our lives in the arts;
   for singers whose voices make our hearts soar;
   for writers whose written word gives us a
      new perspective;
   for musicians who help us hear God's songs;
   for painters whose images give us a new vision.

Thank you, God, for those who, like your Spirit,
   work behind the scenes and out of the spotlight;
   for secretaries who by their work make our
      work better;
   for janitors who clean up after us;
   for medical clerks who keep track of our records;
   for cooks who make our meals.

We thank you, God, for all the ways in which
   the work we do imitates the work you do.
We pray that in our work we may glorify you.
We pray that through our work we may reveal you.
We pray that as we work we may be aware of
   working with you.
Amen.

From Doris Rudy, ed., *Worship and Daily Life: A Resource for Worship Planners*, United Methodist Church, Discipleship Resources, 1999, p. 32.

Study Aids for Use With Chapter One

Objectives

- To understand that we are called to be God's partners in every realm of life, and that taking our faith to work is a key way we fulfill this privilege
- To place the current chasm between faith and work in historical context and learn about efforts to close it
- To recognize why continuing and expanding such efforts is important

Fellowship activity

At the start of this session participants should reintroduce themselves to each other. In doing so, each person should say more about what they now do in their work lives (or did in their last job). Include a word about one of the toughest ethical situations ever faced, as well as about what has been liked most and least in the job.

Questions for discussion

1. Chapter One notes the relative absence today of conversation within workplaces about religion. In *your* workplace do people talk about their religious convictions? Why, or why not? How do you feel about this?

2. Are you accustomed to thinking of yourself as engaging in "ministry" while at work? How does the word "ministry" help you—or not help you— understand the roles God calls you to play in your work life? Do other words (such as "service," or "witness," or "discipleship," or "spirituality") better express your understanding of those roles?

3. What efforts have your denomination and congregation made to close the faith-work gap? Do you see more things that should be done? (Note: If you are unaware of your denomination's efforts in this area, its Web site may offer helpful information and/or insight.)

4. Do you think your workplace is important to God? What do you think God wants for it?

5. In our being Christians at work, how far can we go in sharing our faith with others? What are the different ways of doing so? Have you experienced being able to talk explicitly about the gospel with someone in your workplace? What happened?

6. In your own work experience, have you known people who have appealingly shown a clear connection between their faith and their work? In what specific ways was this connection evident?

7. Are there points made in Chapter One (or in the "Grist" items below) that you think are particularly important and that have not yet been discussed? If so, be sure to raise them with the group.

Grist for further reflection and discussion

"Nothing could be plainer than that if the Christian faith is in the present and future to bring about changes, as it has done in the past, in the thought, habits and practices of society, it can only do this through being the living, working faith of multitudes of lay men and women conducting the ordinary affairs of life . . . . We stand before a great historic task—the task of restoring the lost unity between worship and work."

J. H. Oldham, in the preparatory volume for the 1937 Oxford Conference on Life and Work, cited in Stephen C. Neill and Hans-Ruedi Weber, ed., *The Layman in Christian History* (Westminster Press, 1963), p. 378.

"In the last analysis, the Church speaks to and acts upon the world through her laity. Without a dynamic laity conscious of its personal ministry to the world, the Church, in effect, does not speak or act. No amount of social action by priests and religious can ever be an adequate substitute for enhancing lay responsibility. The absence of lay initiative can only take us down the road to clericalism. We are deeply concerned that so little energy is devoted to encouraging and arousing lay responsibility for the world. The Church must constantly be reformed, but we fear that the almost obsessive preoccupation with the Church's structures and processes has diverted attention from the essential question: reform for what purpose? It would be one of the great ironies of history if the era of Vatican II which opened the windows of the Church to the world were to close with a Church turned in upon herself."

From "The Chicago Declaration of Christian Concern," signed by 47 American Catholic leaders in 1977. Cited in William Droel, *Full-Time Christians: The Real Challenge From Vatican II* (Twenty-Third Publications, 2002), pp. 111-112.

"Mission is primarily and ultimately the work of the Triune God, Creator, Redeemer, and Sanctifier, for the sake of the world, a ministry in which the church is privileged to participate . . . . Mission has its origin in the heart of God. God is a fountain of sending love. This is the deepest source of mission. It is impossible to penetrate deeper still; there is mission because God loves people . . . .

"It is not simply to *receive* life that people are called to become Christians, but rather to *give* life . . . .

"Jesus will not be our Savior if we persistently reject him as Lord of our total life."

Bosch, *Transforming Mission*, pp. 392, 414, 438.

"God assigns some tasks to all people—tasks like going into all the world and communicating the gospel, and loving our neighbors. But when it comes to the specifics—going into a certain part of the world and communicating a particular part of the gospel in a particular way to some particular people at a particular time, or showing love in a specific way to a specific person at a specific time and place—I believe God assigns unique tasks to each of us. I believe that being God's partner means finding out what my particular assignment is and then getting busy carrying it out, using the particular combination of abilities I have.

"God seems to have deliberately set up the world in a way that leaves blanks for human beings to fill . . . . That means that something that needs doing goes undone when I fail to carry out my assignments."

Barbara Wendland, in Wendland and Stanley J. Menking, *God's Partners: Lay Christians at Work* (Judson Press, 1993), p. 20.

For the next time

- Set meeting date and location, leadership responsibilities, and so forth for the next session.
- Read Chapter Two as well as the Study Aids for that chapter. Think through and be prepared to discuss the case study found there. You may wish to share and discuss it with others and bring those insights to the discussion.
- The next session will concentrate on the first two ways Christians can take their faith to work and make a difference there. These are the *ministry of competence* and the *ministry of caring*. In the coming week, look for opportunities to practice these ministries in your workplace.

Closing

The following prayer, called "A Worker's Prayer," may be used at the end of the session. One person reads the bolded lines;

the group reads the rest in unison.

**My work is hard, Lord. I need your counsel
and comfort:**
When things fall apart,
When I'm confronted with evil,
When my co-workers' needs are too great,
When I'm tired to the insides of my brain,
When my work is not appreciated.

**My work is necessary, Lord. I need your gifts
and Spirit:**
When things are developing well,
When I'm making positive changes,
When others' lives have meaning because of my work,
When society is made better because of what I do,
When I'm working efficiently and effectively,
When I'm honored as a valuable worker.

Every day of my work:
I want to remember that you are my God;
I need to know that you're there with me;
I count on your blessings for my successes;
I want to thank you for the chance to work in this place;
I need courage and conviction to see myself as your worker.

For the gifts and your grace that come to me as a worker,
I praise . . . . and thank you.

Amen.

From *Working: Making a Difference in God's World*, A sourcebook
published by the Evangelical Lutheran Church in America, 1995, p. 5/Starters.

Study Aids for Use With Chapter Two

Objectives
- To assess workplace values, both positive and negative, and their implications for our being a Christian at work
- To understand workplace ministries of competence and caring
- To explore ways we can carry out these two ministries

Fellowship activity
At the beginning of this session, brief introductions should include each participant's recalling at least one important point made at the previous session. This might also include participants' present thoughts about things they are especially hoping to change in their own work lives.

Questions for discussion
1. What are the negative values most strongly entrenched in your workplace? The positive ones? Are the negative values now getting stronger or weaker? What are some ways they can be resisted? How risky is such effort for you?

2. The New Testament says God has endowed each of us with certain gifts "for some useful purpose," and "to serve one another." What do you believe are your God-given gifts? In what ways does your current work make good use of those gifts? Are your gifts not being well used in your current work? Do you have other outlets for manifesting them? Do you believe you are in the workplace now where you can best serve God?

3. What can be done to help youngsters move toward a biblical approach to decisions about their work careers? When and how should this get started?

4. Think of the co-worker with whom you have the most difficult interpersonal relationship right now. How much do you know about this person's non-work roles, issues, priorities? Can you think of ways to improve the relationship?

5. What gets in the way of your ministry of caring in the workplace? What can you do about these barriers?

6. Are there points from this chapter not yet talked about that you would like to have discussed? One that you think is particularly important or debatable?

Case study

"Sue had been offered the job of a lifetime. For the past seven years, ever since the death of her husband, she had been working as a service representative at a computer software firm. She was not very happy with the job: few raises, few benefits, and a lot of headaches.

"Today, one of her biggest clients had approached her for a job. They had been so impressed with her recommendations for their business that they wanted her to join their new branch office. Since the job meant moving to the west coast, they had offered Sue a substantial 'signing bonus' and promised her a chance to share in the profits as soon as they got past the start-up stage. Even better, Sue would be in charge of twenty other computer systems employees.

"Sue was only hesitant about one thing: Her two children would not want to leave their high school friends. She was frank about her feelings, and mentioned them to the client at the time he offered the job. He was very understanding. 'Sue,' he said, 'you have to make this decision for yourself. But let me tell you, you are being wasted at this firm. You are bright, intelligent, and you deserve better things. You've sacrificed a lot to raise your family. Now they should sacrifice for you.'"

Laura Nash, *Believers in Business*, p. 289.

- How would you evaluate Sue's situation?
- As a Christian, what are the most important things for her to think about?
- What should be her first step, the next ones?
- If you were in her shoes, what decision do you think you would make? Why?

Grist for further reflection and discussion

"Early Christians did not so much speak of a person going to church, but more often thought of the church as being present with each person at his place of daily employment. To the degree that his work represented the Spirit's call and the Spirit's response, to that extent the Church was actively fulfilling its mission through him."

Paul S. Minear, in Nelson, ed., *Work and Vocation*, p. 67.

"Because our gifts carry us out into the world and make us participants in life, the uncovering of them is one of the most important tasks confronting any one of us . . . . We ask to know the will of God without guessing that his will is written into our very beings. We perceive that will when we discern our gifts. Our obedience and surrender to God are in large part our obedience and surrender to our gifts."

Elizabeth O'Connor, *Eighth Day of Creation: Discovering Your Gifts* (Servant Leadership School, Washington, D.C., 1971), pp. 12, 13.

"Responsible career choice involves the discovery of my talents and abilities, and the location of a place where those talents and abilities can be exercised in the service of others . . . .

[The] question of vocation is more than just the question of paid employment. For the concept of vocation covers our whole life as we relate to God, to other persons, and to creation within the stations, or social roles, that God has placed us. Our work, then, is just one facet of our overall vocation, and it must be integrated with the other facets of our vocation if we are to hear and heed the full scope of God's call within our lives."

Lee Hardy, *The Fabric of This World*, p. 122

"Because there is in you the Glory, as our Lord's passion and resurrection have defined it, there will be in you a deep sensitivity, blended with a deep serenity. In your service of others you will feel, you will care, you will be hurt, you will have your heart broken. And it is doubtful if any of us can do anything at all until we have been very much hurt, and until our hearts have been very much broken. And that is because God's gift to us is the glory of Christ *crucified*—being really sensitive to the pain and sorrow that does exist in so much of the world.

"With this, a serenity that is deep in you—and because it's deep in you it brings to others peace and healing. 'Peace I leave with you. My peace I give unto you.' The life of a Christian ought to be like the ocean, with the surface constantly battered above by storms, but miles and miles below deep peace, unmoved tranquility."

Michael Ramsey, Archbishop of Canterbury, 1963. Quoted in Mark Gibbs and T. Ralph Morton, *God's Frozen People*, pp. 186-187.

For the next time

- Set meeting date and location, leadership responsibilities, and so forth for the next session.
- Read Chapter Three together with the Study Aids in preparation. Be prepared to discuss the case study found there. You may wish to share and discuss it with others and bring their insights to the discussion.

- The next session will cover the *ministry of ethics* and the *ministry of change*. In the coming week, look for opportunities to practice these ministries in your workplace.

Closing

This adaptation of St. Teresa's prayer, said aloud by all participants, could be a fitting close to the session:

Lord, I know that Christ has no body on earth but ours, no hands but ours, no feet but ours; ours are the eyes through which Christ looks out in compassion to the world, ours are the feet with which he is to go about doing good, and ours are the hands with which he is to bless the world now.

Lord, Make it so in my life, now and always. Amen.

Study Aids for Use With Chapter Three

Objectives
- To understand the ministry of ethics and explore how it can be carried out in our workplaces
- To understand the ministry of change and share ideas about how we as individuals can make contributions to positive change in our workplaces

Fellowship activity
As participants go around the circle and reintroduce themselves at the beginning, it could be helpful for each person to recall one important new thought about the faith-work connection that came to them at the previous session.

Questions for discussion
1. Do you believe that "distinguishing between right and wrong" is more difficult today than in the past? Is it any more difficult in workplaces than in other realms of life? What can we do to be clearer about right and wrong in the workplace? To be strong enough to do the right?

2. Have you ever found yourself in a situation where your boss or someone in authority asked you to do something you thought was unethical, and you did what you were told? How did you feel about it? If this happens again in the future, what possibilities do you see for acting differently?

3. What are the implications of the gospel for the secretary who is told to tell a caller (falsely) that her boss is not in? For the other people mentioned in the

same paragraph (page 53-54)? What would you do in each of these cases? Why?

4. Have you ever thought of the organization where you work in relation to God's kingdom? How does your organization serve the kingdom? Get in its way? What would need to be changed to make your organization better reflect the kingdom value of economic justice? How can this be done?

5. Are there "roving leader" roles you play in your workplace? What additional possibilities do you see for you to carry out a ministry of change in your place of work?

6. What is the prevailing understanding of work in your organization? Does it come closer to being a glorification or a vilification of work? Is change on this front desirable? Possible? What would you like to see happen? What can you do to help make it happen?

7. Are there points from this chapter not yet talked about that you would like to have discussed?

Case study

Beth is a young attorney in her first job out of law school. Her law firm is involved in the defense of a contractor being sued by a group of homeowners for defective construction. While taking depositions, Beth is with Ben, an older lawyer in the firm. As Beth observes him interrogating one of the homeowners, she is disturbed by the deliberate way he seeks to confuse the witness and put him on the defensive. To her, Ben's manner seems abusive. As a Christian, she knows it violates her sense of ethical responsibility.

At the end of the day, when Beth gently raises the issue with Ben, his response is immediate. "Don't be naïve, Beth.

Our job is to defend the construction company. We need to discredit the testimony of the homeowners. You're going to have to learn that, too, if you're going to get anywhere in this firm."

Beth wanted to do well in her job, and she knew that she would be the person doing the interrogation the next day. She knew that treating people this way did not fit her understanding of what it means to be a person of faith. But she was hired to defend the contractor, and she wanted to win the case. She wondered how she would proceed.

Adapted from a case developed by the Council for Ethics in Economics, Columbus, Ohio

- What options do you believe Beth has?
- What course of action do you think she should take? Why?

Grist for further reflection and discussion

"For the Christian community, ethics are part and parcel of its witness in the world. Our service to others in love calls attention to God's self-giving love in Jesus Christ. The values we seek, we seek because they are values God has promised to realize, in their fullness, in the fullness of God's coming reign. We have a vision of what those values are in the vision of that future dominion of God that is revealed in Jesus' resurrection victory over sin and death. To seek these goods, then, witnesses to the hope that is within us and anticipates the things God has promised."

James M. Childs, Jr., *Ethics in Business: Faith at Work*, p. 26.

"The challenging and comprehensive contribution of Christianity to the ethical conduct of business is not the delivery of a series of arbitrary moral injunctions. It is an exploring within the realm of business of the practical consequences of those beliefs about God and humanity that Christians hold as their distinctive way of interpreting and construing human existence. It unashamedly asks ultimate questions about the purpose of life and of human society, and about the intrinsic purpose of business as one among many expressions of social relationships and activities. It also claims to offer answers to such questions in ways that do not just satisfy intellectual curiosity, but that have . . . behavioral implications for business activity at all levels."

Jack Mahoney, S.J., in Paul M. Minus, ed., *The Ethics of Business in a Global Economy* (Kluwer Academic Publishers, 1993), p. 115.

"We don't need work to be whole, fulfilled human beings—there has been too much exaggerated sentiment sold us . . . about the fulfilling meaning of work . . . . Work becomes one place of many in which I play out who I am, rather than the place in which I discover and prove who I am. Work is not fraught with the power to make or break me; succeeding or failing at work, being appreciated or disappointed over work, is just that, not more."

James E. Dittes, *Men at Work: Life Beyond the Office* (Westminster John Knox Press, 1996), pp. 8, 90.

"Even with all its failings, work must be saved . . . . Work must be recast to fit the needs of both individuals and the communities of which they are a part. Work must recapture its true purpose: To produce products people need and to help produce better people."

Al Gini, *My Job, My Self: Work and the Creation of the Modern Individual* (Routledge, 2000), p. 209.

For the next time

- Set meeting date and location, leadership responsibilities, and so forth for the next session.
- Read Chapter Four together with the Study Aids in preparation. You may wish to share and discuss it with others and bring their insights to the discussion.
- The next session will cover how as individuals and congregations we can sustain and expand efforts to

overcome the Sunday-Monday disconnect. In the coming week, consider the role you can play in this task.

Closing

This affirmation of faith might be said in unison at the end of the session, perhaps with brief prayers added from participants.

We believe in God, the Creator of this amazing universe, who continues to make all things new. From new galaxies to the birth of a child, from new learning and discoveries in science to the arrival of spring after a difficult winter, God is creating. We believe, O Creator God, that you are constantly weaving the fiber of goodness within the world.

We believe in Jesus Christ, the Savior of this world, who shows the way for living life to its full potential. It is Christ who leads us to seek forgiveness and conveys through his life and death the immense love of God available to all. It is Christ who asks us to have the hearts of little children and to trust and love God wholly and to love our neighbor as ourselves. We believe, O Christ, that you are constantly calling us to be transformed to your likeness.

We believe in the Holy Spirit, the presence of God daily in our lives, the Spirit of truth, justice, and love, who guides and informs us, and the comforting attendant who holds us when we are passing through dark valleys. Joy, patience, compassion—all come from the Holy Spirit. We believe, O Spirit of God, that you seek to be present in every dimension of our lives.

O triune God, may we know you fully and may our lives glorify you. Amen.

From Doris Rudy, ed., *Worship and Daily Life: A Resource for Worship Planners*, United Methodist Church, Discipleship Resources, 1999, p. 43.

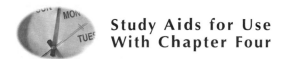

Study Aids for Use With Chapter Four

Objectives
- To share ideas about how we as individuals can stay focused on God's call and persist in building our workplace ministry
- To explore a more active role for our congregation in evoking and supporting workplace ministry

Fellowship activity
As this final session begins, it may be helpful for each person to say something about what new learning or resolve has been most important to them as they have read and reflected about Chapter Four.

Questions for discussion
1. What other person (or group) do you most rely upon for personal support as you face the challenges of your workplace? How effective is this support for you? Are there ways it can be strengthened?

2. Do you ever pray at work? If so, when, where, how? What steps are possible to help you step back and take reflective time, especially to think about ways your own ministry at work can be more deliberate and effective?

3. What grade would you give the institutional church in general for supporting people's work lives? What grade would you give your congregation?

4. What can your congregation do to more effectively awaken and support members' workplace ministries?

What can this group or you do to move the congregation in this direction?

5. Imagine you have been asked to talk with young clergy about what they can do to help people better serve Christ in their work lives. What would you say to them?

6. Are there points from this chapter not yet talked about that you would like to be discussed?

7. As the members of the group individually and collectively think about where this study of *Taking Faith to Work* will take them next, consider these possibilities:

- Is there interest in continuing this group in some way? Perhaps meeting less frequently, more frequently?
- Are there people in the same occupation within the congregation who would be interested in organizing a continuing discussion focused on how the gospel relates to their work's unique issues and challenges?
- Do you have an interest in connecting with an organization such as the Forum for Faith in the Workplace, or the Coalition for Ministry in Daily Life, which provide continuing contact with scattered individuals and groups? If so, both organizations (and others as well) can be reached through the Coalition's Web site: www.dailylifeministry.org.

Grist for further reflection and study

"Without deliberate planning and certainly without any nefarious scheming on the part of the clergy, the congregation has developed a structure that depends entirely on the minister. The life of the congregation has grown up around him and depends on him, and it does not matter whether he is called priest or pastor, rector or minister. His central position has determined the organizations and activities of the congregation and the nature of its piety. This is seen as so natural that most people will say that it is only right; that this is why you have ministers at all; that this is their job; for this they are trained. But for all that, this is what is crippling the life of the church."

Mark Gibbs and R. Ralph Morton, *God's Frozen People*, p. 49.

"I have good news for pastors who support the principle of every member in ministry but who are afraid to encourage it for fear that there will be less support for the survival needs of the congregation. I have never encountered a congregation whose people were engaged in Ministry in Daily Life that was not also a thriving congregation . . . . The reason is simple: As members seek to carry out their ministries in daily life, they always return to their churches, the places for recharging their spiritual batteries. Through Word and Sacrament, education, and support groups, members of a congregation are renewed for weekday ministry in the world."

William E. Diehl, *Ministry in Daily Life*, pp. 8-9.

Closing

The following "Act of Commitment to Vocation in Daily Life" may be an appropriate way for the group to conclude its final session.

Leader: My brothers and sisters in Christ Jesus: We are all baptized by one Spirit into one body, and given gifts for a variety of ministries for the common good. In the ministry of your daily life and work, will you proclaim by word and example the Good News of God in Christ?

People: I will.

Leader: In your daily occupation, will you seek and serve Christ in all persons, loving your neighbor as yourself?

People: I will.

Leader: In the vocation to which God has called you, will you strive for justice and peace among all people, and respect the dignity of every human being?

People: I will.

Leader: Name the occupation for which you seek God's blessing.

People: (Each person names his or her occupation.)

Leader: Let us pray. Almighty God, whose Son Jesus Christ in his earthly life shared our toil and hallowed our labor: Be present with your people where they work. Deliver us from the service of self alone, and grant that we, remembering the account that we must one day give, may be faithful stewards of your good gifts; for the sake of him who came among us as one who serves, your Son our Savior Jesus Christ.

People: Amen.

Leader: In the name of God and of this congregation, I recognize and affirm your commitment to follow Christ in the places and tasks to which God has called you. May the Holy Spirit guide and strengthen you to bear faithful witness to Christ, and to carry on his holy work in the world.

People: Amen.

Adapted from the original form, which was developed by Episcopal priest J. Fletcher Lowe, Jr., and which is found in Linda L. Grenz and Lowe, eds., *Ministry in Daily Life: A Guide to Living the Baptismal Covenant*, pp. 140-141.

Selected Bibliography

Seminal Volumes
These six books appeared during the surge of interest in lay vocation and ministry that occurred during the 1950s and 1960s. They continue to be valuable.

Congar, Yves M. J., *Lay People in the Church: A Study for a Theology of the Laity.* London: Geoffrey Chapman and Westminster, Maryland: Christian Classics, 1985.
This volume, by a pioneering French Catholic theologian, was originally published in France in 1951 and subsequently went through several revisions and editions. It delves deeply into the church's traditional thought and practice, from a perspective greatly influenced by St. Thomas Aquinas.

Gibbs, Mark and Morton, T. Ralph, *God's Frozen People: A Book For and About Christian Laymen.* Philadelphia: Westminster Press, 1965.
Written by a British layman and clergyman, this book contains a sharp but loving critique of the church's failure to recognize the place of laity in the vanguard of the Christian mission in the world.

Kraemer, Hendrik, *A Theology of the Laity.* Philadelphia: Westminster Press, 1958.
The author was a Dutch theologian and missionary leader creatively concerned about the church's interaction with the modern world. He believed the laity's place in this interaction is critical.

Neill, Stephen Charles and Weber, Hans-Ruedi, eds., *The Layman in Christian History: A Project of the Department on the Laity of the World Council of Churches.* Philadelphia: Westminster Press, 1963.
Seventeen essays, most of them by prominent church historians, explore the ways the laity's role has been understood throughout Christian history. Neill was a bishop in the Church of South India, Weber a leader for laity issues within the World Council of Churches.

Nelson, John Oliver, ed., *Work and Vocation: A Christian Discussion.* New York: Harper & Brothers, 1954.

This book contains perceptive essays by five American scholars involved in a study commissioned by the World Council of Churches. The editor was a long-time teacher and administrator at the Yale Divinity School.

Trueblood, Elton, *Your Other Vocation.* New York, Harper & Brothers, 1952.

This little book was an early statement by Trueblood, a widely influential American Quaker philosopher, about a theme central to his understanding of Christianity.

Theological Studies

The many theological volumes available for further study include the following seven books written by authors from a variety of traditions and perspectives.

Bosch, David J., *Transforming Mission: Paradigm Shifts in a Theology of Mission.* Maryknoll, New York: Orbis Books, 1991.

Bosch was a Protestant missiologist who taught for many years in his native South Africa. This book, while not focusing chiefly on issues of lay ministry, does provide a pertinent analysis of the church's shifting understandings through history of its mission in the world.

Childs, James M., Jr., *Ethics in Business: Faith at Work.* Minneapolis: Fortress Press, 1995.

Childs, an American Lutheran seminary teacher and administrator, has been constructively involved with Christian business leaders at the intersection of ethics and economics. His knowledge of these issues is evident in this book.

Hardy, Lee, *The Fabric of This World: Inquiries into Calling, Career Choice, and the Design of Human Work.* Grand Rapids, Michigan: William B. Eerdmans Publishing Company, 1990.

Hardy brings to this study an unusual combination of theological insight (from a Reformed perspective) and appreciation for practical issues of job design and choice. He is a professor of philosophy at Calvin College in Michigan.

Haughey, John C., *Converting Nine to Five: Bringing Spirituality to Your Daily Work.* New York: Crossroad Publishing Company, 1994.

Haughey, an American Catholic scholar, focuses his Jesuit/Ignatian theological perspective on many practical issues encountered in the workplace.

Mead, Loren B., *The Once and Future Church: Reinventing the Congregation for a New Mission Frontier.* Washington, D. C.: The Alban Institute, Inc. 1991.

With great conceptual clarity and practical wisdom this little book analyzes what must be done for the renewal of congregations. Mead, an American Episcopal priest, believes that the laity will have the key role in the renewed church's outreach to the world.

Stevens, R. Paul, *The Other Six Days: Vocation, Work, and Ministry in Biblical Perspective.* Grand Rapids, Michigan: William B. Eerdmans Publishing Company, 2000.

Stevens, an Evangelical theologian and pastor, brings to this book long experience with both conceptual and practical issues of workplace ministry. He is professor of applied theology at Regent College in Vancouver.

Volf, Miroslav, *Work in the Spirit: Toward a Theology of Work.* New York: Oxford University Press, 1991.

Volf develops a fresh theological understanding of work moving beyond the widely influential one articulated by Luther. A native of Croatia, Volf now teaches at the Yale Divinity School.

Practical Steps for Individuals and Congregations

These books present a rich assortment of stories and experience from Christians actively engaged in the movement to connect faith and work.

Banks, Robert J., ed., *Faith Goes to Work: Reflections from the Marketplace.* Washington, D. C.: The Alban Institute, Inc. 1993.

Most of the fourteen essays in this book are written by people involved in lay ministry in the workplace. The editor, an Australian, taught at Fuller Theological Seminary and has published widely on the connection between faith and everyday life.

Chappell, Tom, *The Soul of a Business: Managing for Profit and the Common Good.* New York: Bantam Books, 1993.

Chappell is an Episcopal layman who describes the effort to run his business, Tom's of Maine, in the light of his faith.

De Pree, Max, *Leadership Is an Art.* New York: Dell Publishing, 1989.

De Pree's thoughts about leadership, developed over many years as CEO of a Fortune 500 company based in Michigan, are clearly influenced by his Christian faith.

Diehl, William E., *Ministry in Daily Life: A Practical Guide to Congregations.* Bethesda, Maryland: The Alban Institute, Inc. 1996.

This little book is full of practical suggestions that emerged from the Lutheran church in Pennsylvania where Diehl was a member for many years.

Diehl, William E., *The Monday Connection: On Being an Authentic Christian in a Weekday World.* San Francisco: HarperSanFrancisco, 1991.

Diehl's experience as a steel executive was the setting for the emergence of a rich understanding of how he could bring his faith to bear on his workplace responsibilities. This book combines a strong conceptual framework with numerous stories from daily life.

Dozier,Verna, ed., *The Calling of the Laity.*
Washington, D. C.: The Alban Institute, Inc. 1988.
The two-dozen essays collected here provide unusual insight into varied issues facing lay disciples, some of them arising in workplaces, some in congregations. Dozier was a school teacher for many years in the District of Columbia.

Droel, William L., *The Spirituality of Work: Business People.* Chicago: ACTA Publications, 1991.
Droel, a Catholic layman and leader of the National Center for the Laity, has also written (and helped others write) similar booklets for people who are visual artists, homemakers, lawyers, military personnel, nurses, teachers, and unemployed.

Jacobsen, Steve, *Hearts to God, Hands to Work: Connecting Spirituality and Work.* Bethesda, Maryland: The Alban Institute, Inc. 1997.
Jacobsen's pastorate in a Presbyterian church in California was preceded by experience in several secular workplaces. His book contains many practical suggestions for helping congregations make the Sunday-Monday connection.

Nash, Laura L., *Believers in Business.* Nashville: Thomas Nelson Publishers, 1994.
Nash, a business ethicist, explores numerous dimensions of the faith-work connection practiced by Evangelical business leaders.

Pierce, Gregory F. A., ed., *Of Human Hands: A Reader in the Spirituality of Work.* Minneapolis: Augsburg and Chicago: ACTA, 1991.
Pierce, a Catholic layman and publisher, brings together twenty short essays describing the authors' personal efforts to serve God in a variety of workplaces.

Pierce, Gregory F. A., *spirituality@work: 10 ways to balance your life on-the-job.* Chicago: Loyola Press, 2001.
Pierce here shows how Christians can find God in the workplace as they seek to combine faith and work.

Rudy, Doris, ed., *Worship and Daily Life: A Resource for Worship Planners.* Nashville: Discipleship Resources of the United Methodist Church, 1999.

Rudy and ten other liturgical writers have created previously unpublished resources for congregational worship, including a wide range of greetings, confessions, affirmations of faith, and prayers – all of them focused on Christians' daily interaction with the world.

Weiser, Carol L., ed., *Working: Making a Difference in God's World.* Chicago: Evangelical Lutheran Church in America, 1995.

Lutheran leaders here bring together a rich assortment of resources, personal stories, and practical suggestions from numerous workplaces and congregations.

About the Author

P aul M. Minus is a retired United Methodist clergyman who currently serves as president of the Coalition for Ministry in Daily Life (www.dailylifeministry.org), an international network of Christians and their organizations. He and his wife Jean live in Massachusetts.

After receiving his Ph.D. in 1962, Paul served two years as University Chaplain at Florida State University. He then taught for twenty-five years at the Methodist Theological School in Ohio. In his final workplace role before retiring, he was founding president of the Council for Ethics in Economics, located in Columbus, Ohio.

This is his sixth book. Previous ones include *The Catholic Rediscovery of Protestantism* (1976), *Walter Rauschenbusch: American Reformer* (1988), and *The Ethics of Business in a Global Economy* (1993).